D1739689

SOCIAL WORK AND LAW

COHABITATION

AUSTRALIA
The Law Book Company Ltd.
Sydney : Melbourne : Brisbane

CANADA AND U.S.A.
The Carswell Company Ltd.
Agincourt, Ontario

INDIA
N.M. Tripathi Private Ltd.
Bombay
and
Eastern Law House Private Ltd.
Calcutta
M.P.P. House
Bangalore

ISRAEL
Steimatzky's Agency Ltd.
Jerusalem : Tel Aviv : Haifa

MALAYSIA : SINGAPORE : BRUNEI
Malayan Law Journal (Pte.) Ltd.
Singapore

NEW ZEALAND
Sweet and Maxwell (N.Z.) Ltd.
Auckland

PAKISTAN
Pakistan Law House
Karachi

SOCIAL WORK AND LAW

COHABITATION

by

MARTIN L. PARRY, LL.B.

Solicitor, Lecturer in Law at the University of Hull

With a foreword by
PROFESSOR H. K. BEVAN

LONDON
SWEET & MAXWELL
1981

Published in 1981 by
Sweet & Maxwell Limited of
11 New Fetter Lane, London
Computerset by
MFK Graphic Systems (Typesetting) Limited
Saffron Walden, Essex
Printed in Great Britain by
Thomson Litho Limited
East Kilbride, Scotland

British Library Cataloguing in Publication Data

Parry, Martin L
    Cohabitation. – (Social work and law).
    1. Unmarried couples – Legal status, laws, etc. –
    Great Britain
    I. Title   II. Series
    344.1061'6   KD753

ISBN 0-421-26730-5

FOREWORD

A review of the law concerning the family over the past three decades reveals a pattern of changing emphases. In the fifties (and earlier) concentration was primarily on the matrimonial offence, as the law reports amply demonstrate. The sixties and seventies, influenced markedly by the work of the Law Commission, saw a shift to what inveterately, but inaccurately, were referred to as the "ancillary remedies" of financial provision for members of the family and custody and cognate matters affecting its children. In the seventies, too, public concern for the fate of children of broken homes loomed large, with increasingly complex laws allowing inroads into parental rights. It may confidently be predicted that the subject of this book will command significant attention in the eighties. Mr. Parry's treatment of it should do much to achieve that result, for such has been the growth in recent years of the legal recognition accorded to relationships outside marriage that the spasmodic appearance of legal commentary to which it once gave rise will no longer suffice.

This does not mean that a monograph can compositely and coherently cover the law affecting all extra-marital relationships. The author has wisely eschewed any attempt to do so, preferring to concentrate very largely on the legal consequences that arise from "cohabitation between a man and a woman living together as husband and wife" (p. 9). Even within that relationship recognition has been pragmatic and there emerges neither statutory nor judicial consistency of approach. The author's own approach properly reflects this pragmatism, but I venture to suggest that this new and careful examination of the subject will encourage attempts to formulate a basis for legal recognition, whether it be found in the concept of status or of contract or of dependence.

The book appears as one in the series for social workers. Mr. Parry has them primarily and constantly in mind and I certainly commend it to them. Its lucidity and content will, however, appeal to a wider readership. In particular I commend it to the practitioner and the student of law, both of whom will also find it of immense benefit.

Hugh Bevan
Professor of Law

University of Hull

PREFACE

Increasing attention is being paid to the legal rights and obligations of unmarried couples. This book has been written to meet the needs of those with an involvement or interest in the subject and is aimed primarily at those engaged in the social services, whether as practitioners or students. It is hoped that it will be of use also to advisory bodies as well as lawyers, law students and laymen. With the needs of practitioners in mind, the text includes the citation of cases, statutes and other authorities, which may not be of interest to the general reader.

The title *Cohabitation* has been chosen to describe the relationship of unmarried couples who live together as husband and wife. Consideration is also given to relationships which do not amount to cohabitation in that sense, for example, where members of a family live together in a relationship of companionship.

I have been helped considerably in the preparation of the book by a number of colleagues. In particular, special thanks are due to Professor Hugh Bevan for his inspiration and encouragement throughout and for his help in reading through the entire manuscript, a task which my wife Deborah has also willingly undertaken and for which I thank her. Help on individual chapters has been forthcoming from Professor Paul Fairest, Mr. Nicholas Parry and Mr. Tony Prosser, and with materials from Mr. Stephen Cretney of the Law Commission. No doubt errors and omissions remain, but responsibility for them is entirely mine. My thanks go also to Mrs. Valerie Kelly for deciphering and typing the manuscript at short notice.

Discussion is limited to the law in England and Wales and I have tried to state the law as at February 1, 1981, although I have referred where appropriate to statutory changes which are not yet in operation. As always the law changes almost before the ink has dried on the page.

University of Hull   Martin Parry

CONTENTS

TABLE OF CASES

TABLE OF STATUTES

FOREIGN STATUTES

1 Introduction

"It is, I think, not putting it too high to say that between 1950 and 1975 there has been a complete revolution in society's attitude to unmarried partnerships." (Bridge L.J. in *Dyson Holdings Ltd.* v. *Fox* (1975).)
To what extent has the law matched this revolution? Our society is based on the family unit centred on marriage. The law has encouraged marriage and discouraged cohabitation. Yet the law also reflects society's views and, as unions outside marriage are becoming more socially acceptable, so the law is beginning to give recognition, albeit limited, to such relationships.

TERMINOLOGY

It is necessary at the outset to define cohabitation. "To cohabit" generally means to live together as husband and wife, and is usually used of persons who are not married. "Cohabitation" describes the relationship of a couple who cohabit and they are frequently referred to as "cohabitees."

The term "cohabitee" is, however, grammatically irregular. Yet an alternative is not easy to find. "Cohabitant" is correct but too much of a mouthful. "Concubine," in respect of a woman, is correct but technical. Reported American alternatives include "meaningful associate," "special friend," "current companion" and "domestic associate," none of which, it is suggested, is helpful or meaningful. Various judicial alternatives may be appropriate for the law reports but not for everday use; for example, "illegitimate wife and illegitimate husband," "family partner," "*de facto* spouse," "unmarried housewife." In popular use are "common law wife" and "mistress," both of which are expressive but inaccurate. In the absence of any better alternative it is proposed to use the term "cohabitee" when referring to what the Department of Health and Social Security describes as those who are living together as husband and wife.

The terms "common law husband" and "common law wife" are misleading and their use is not to be encouraged, for they suggest a particular kind of legal relationship which in fact does not exist. The

1

terms arose when marriage law was a part of ecclesiastical law and there were strict penalties for sexual relationships outside marriage. At common law, however, no religious ceremony was necessary, parties could marry by merely declaring that they took each other as husband and wife or by declaring an intention to do so, in which case the marriage was binding when the parties had sexual intercourse (*i.e.* consummated the marriage). The rule was later modified so that a marriage was valid only if conducted in the presence of a priest, but the law was in a state of uncertainty until the Marriage Act 1753. That Act, which is the basis of the modern law of formation of marriage, removed the common law marriage and required a church ceremony after the calling of banns, the consent of a minor's parents or guardians and the entry of the ceremony in an official register. Later legislation permitted marriage by civil ceremony.

Common law marriages can still be contracted in other countries, for example in certain parts of the United States of America. In Scotland such marriages were effective until the Marriage (Scotland) Act 1939. Indeed, it is still possible in Scotland to have a marriage "by cohabitation with habit and repute" where a couple have set up home together and live together as husband and wife. The Marriage (Scotland) Act 1977, s. 21 provides for the registration of such "irregular marriages." Certain customs, similar to the common law marriage, were followed by wandering groups, particularly in the north of England, to gain social acceptability for relationships outside marriage. One such custom was the marriage over the broom (or living over the brush) where the group provided its own ceremony in which the couple joined hands and jumped over a broom which was swung in circles near the ground.

The term "mistress" is often used synonymously with cohabitee but the two are not the same. Nor are the legal rights respectively attaching to them. Mistress suggests a woman who has been provided with a home by a man so that he may visit her and enjoy a sexual relationship (see for example *Horrocks* v. *Forray* (1976), *post*, p. 27) and it will be used in that context hereafter. The relationship of mistress and lover is not that of husband and wife nor can it be described as one of cohabitation. The legal recognition of relationships outside marriage has concentrated on couples who have lived as married couples and the preparedness to extend to cohabitees certain legal protection enjoyed by spouses has not been accorded to mistresses. For example, matrimonial injunctions under the Domestic Violence and Matrimonial Proceedings Act 1976, s. 1 (see Chapter 4) apply to "a man and a woman who are living with each other in the same household as husband and wife" and not to mistresses. In the words of one Law Lord they apply to "the unmarried housewife." A cohabitee may be described as an unmarried housewife but the description does not include a mistress. Moreover, the term cohabitee describes both partners of the relationship; mistress clearly does not. Yet if recognition is to be given to a relationship is it realistic to talk just in terms of one partner? It may be difficult, of course, in a particular case to determine whether a woman is a cohabitee or a mistress; for example the woman with whom a man lives from Monday to Friday to be near his job, the man leaving to live with his wife at weekends.

It seems that it is those relationships which can be defined in terms of marriage which are receiving legal recognition. There is a tendency therefore for cohabitees to be defined in terms of spouses as, for example, in the Consumer Credit Act 1974, s. 184, where references to a husband and wife include a "reputed husband or wife." (See likewise "reputed spouse" in the Pneumoconiosis, etc. (Workers' Compensation) Act 1979, *post*, p. 98.)

The tendency to define cohabitees in terms of spouses is consistent with the tendency to presume that a couple living together are married. Thus in *Re Taplin* (1937) a couple lived together for 10 years and held themselves out as husband and wife. They and their children were received into local society. The children's birth certificates recorded the marriage of their parents but there was no record in the appropriate register of marriages and there was a reference in a deed of covenant by the children's paternal grandfather to his son's "reputed children." The court held that the absence of any entry in the register of marriages, and the words in the deed of covenant, were insufficient to rebut the presumption of marriage.

The legal definition of cohabitation depends upon the qualitative and quantitative nature of the cohabitation and the purpose for which it is being claimed, or denied, that a couple are cohabiting. A distinction is drawn, for example, between short term and long term cohabitation, between the casual affair and the stable relationship, between relationships which have resulted in the birth of children and those which have not, and between couples who live together and couples who do not.

For certain purposes the legal test is one of financial dependency rather than cohabitation (see, for example, the Inheritance (Provision for Family and Dependants) Act 1975, *post*, Chapter 5). A mistress might well be dependent upon her lover notwithstanding the lack of cohabitation (see, for example, *Malone* v. *Harrison* (1979), *post*, p. 86). When considering the legal position outside marriage it will be essential therefore to consider not only the nature of the relationship, but also the particular legal issues arising from that relationship.

Where the relationship is no more than a casual encounter there is unlikely to be either cohabitation or dependency and the relationship is unlikely to warrant special recognition. To give it that would defeat one of the objects of such a relationship, namely, the lack of commitments. The difficulty remains, however, of where to draw the line between the stable union and the casual encounter.

Cohabitation can be seen as an informal contract just as marriage is a formal contract and each gives rise to its own status. The protection of matrimonial law does not extend to those who cohabit, but they can be properly described as members of a family. It was said by one Court of Appeal judge in 1950 that:

"To say of two people masquerading as husband and wife that they were members of the same family, seems to me an abuse of the English language."

Yet in the same court a quarter of a century later it was said that:

"The ordinary man would certainly say that the parties to such a union, provided it had the appropriate degree of apparent permanence and stability, were members of a single family."

There remains the problem of defining the appropriate degree of permanence and stability. While marriage in itself usually creates a family, its existence is no longer regarded, either by the courts or by Parliament, as a prerequisite to the creation of a family (see, for example, *Dyson Holdings Ltd.* v. *Fox* (1975), *post*, p. 92 and the Family Income Supplements Act 1970, *post*, p. 49). The judicial and legislative approaches have been tentative and piecemeal, the matter being considered very much in individual contexts.

There is a need for a comprehensive definition of the family and a reappraisal of the role of family law in the light of the current assessment of family ties, so that those who live together outside marriage can be advised with some degree of certainty whether or not they do so as a family. If they are a family should they not get the protection of family law? It has been argued that "Family law should encourage individual fulfilment in the development of personal relationships where this involves marital, quasi-marital or parental roles and provide an adjustment process on the reorientation of these relationships." (Eekelaar 1975.)

OCCURRENCE

Marriage is self proving, cohabitation is not. There is a register of marriages but not of cohabitations so there are no statistics, as such, on the incidence of cohabitation. The increase in the divorce rate (162,450 divorce petitions filed in 1978 compared with 54,036 in 1968) as a result of divorce reform (see Chapter 7) has not been matched by a decrease in cohabitation. One of the objects of the reformed law was to enable those who were unable to marry to regularise by marriage their "stable illicit unions" (see *Field of Choice*, paras. 33–37). This object was realised in the short term but not in the long term.

The frequency of cohabitation, like the frequency of divorce, suggests a decline in the popularity and permanence of marriage, but there is insufficient evidence to do more than speculate on the actual incidence of cohabitation. In recent years there has been a decline in the marriage rate, but it is not suggested that cohabitation is becoming a replacement for, rather than an alternative to, marriage. 357,000 marriages took place in England and Wales in 1977 and there are over 12 million married couples in England and Wales. Marriage continues to be the basis of our social pattern.

Some indication of the frequency of cohabitation resulting in the birth of children may be gained from the registration of illegitimate births. In 1966 38 per cent. of illegitimate births were registered on the joint application of both parents. Ten years later, this figure had risen to 51 per cent. It can be argued from these figures that as the fathers were prepared to acknowledge paternity there is a strong likelihood that in many cases the father and mother were living together.

These figures give no indication, of course, of the incidence of cohabitation without the birth of children, on which any speculation is even more tentative. It does seem, however, that cohabitation is on the increase and there is evidence that increasing numbers of couples cohabit before marriage in what have come to be called trial marriages. Cohabitation is likely to remain an alternative to marriage and may increase in attraction if the proposal of the Law Commission, that the status of illegitimacy be abolished, becomes law (Chapter 6). An increase in cohabitation may in turn result in a decline in divorce if it is accepted as socially, as well as legally, unnecessary to dissolve a marriage before cohabiting.

COMPARISON WITH MARRIAGE

English family law is based on the legal rights and duties arising from marriage. The law regards cohabitation and the sharing of lives and a home as the essence of marriage and recognises rights and duties arising from cohabitation within marriage (see *post*, p. 133). Parties who cohabit outside marriage do not have the legal responsibilities of a married couple. Nor do the benefits and burdens of matrimonial law extend to them. This is so because our social structure is based on marriage, a formal contract giving rise to a particular status. Marriage has been defined as "the voluntary union for life of one man and one woman to the exclusion of all others" (Lord Penzance in *Hyde* v. *Hyde* (1866)), a form of words still used by many registrars of marriage.

It is not possible to enter into a contract of marriage except in accordance with the formalities of the Marriage Acts. The parties are not free to choose the terms of the contract and any private agreement to live together (as, for example, in the American case of *Peck* v. *Peck* (1892)) will not be a marriage. Moreover, it is likely that any contract to cohabit would be regarded as an immoral contract and thus illegal (see Chapter 8).

Cohabitation without marriage is regarded by many people, including many judges, as immoral. The acceptance of marriage as the basis of our social structure inevitably means that the law will differentiate between marriage and cohabitation. Yet increased recognition is being given to cohabitation as for example in the cohabitation rule for social security purposes (see Chapter 3), so that cohabitation, like marriage, is giving rise to a particular status.

Marriage does, of course, impose duties as well as confer rights, although there is a tendency to talk solely in terms of rights, but to do so is inaccurate for rights usually go hand in hand with duties. One of the attractions of cohabitation is that it does not impose upon the parties the duties imposed by marriage. The more the law recognises cohabitation and confers rights on cohabitees the more it will be inclined to impose obligations upon them and the more their freedom of choice is infringed. It is not readily apparent how many couples cohabit through choice and how many are not free to marry. The reform of the divorce law has made remarriage easier and would suggest that the need to cohabit because of an existing marriage of one of the parties is not as great as previously. In some cases it may be that the parties are free to marry but only one of them wishes to do so. If a couple live together because they have chosen not to marry, is it right that the law should treat them as if they were married? In the words of Sir George Baker, former President of the Family Division of the Supreme Court:

> "Should we perhaps pause to ask ourselves whether, and how, marriage can be made more, not less, attractive in its material consequences?"

Is it not time perhaps for a review not only of marriage but also of cohabitation?

Detailed consideration of the legal consequences of marriage and cohabitation must be left until the following chapters when specific issues are discussed and marriage and cohabitation are contrasted. While the common law doctrine of unity, whereby spouses were treated as one person with that one being the husband, is that of a bygone age, its ghost still haunts certain areas of the law relating to husband and wife (see Chapter 8). It is visible in the practice of a woman taking the surname of her husband on marriage. There is, however, no legal requirement that she should do so. People are free to be known by whatever surname they choose, provided that they do not choose one for a fraudulent purpose. A married woman can retain her maiden name if she so wishes and a cohabitee can use his or her own surname or that of the partner. No legal formalities are necessary, but are available should it be felt necessary ever to prove the change of name.

Whilst some of our law has been extended to cohabitees, for example in matters of property (Chapter 2), domestic violence (Chapter 4) and on death (Chapter 5), matrimonial law by its nature is limited to married couples. Thus, the courts' wide and complex discretionary powers on breakdown of marriage (see Chapter 7) are not available on breakdown of cohabitation. It may be argued that cohabitees should be entitled to the same legal protection as married people. Yet is it right that those who choose not to enter into matrimony should be entitled to the protection of matrimonial law? The parties may have chosen to cohabit in order not to be subject to the complex provisions of matrimonial law.

The legal recognition of marriage means that certain relatives are prohibited by law from marrying. The prohibited degrees of affinity which arise from marriage do not attach to cohabitation. Whereas a man may not marry his wife's mother or wife's daughter he is quite free to marry his cohabitee's mother or cohabitee's daughter (see, for example, *Wing* v. *Taylor* (1861)). Cohabitation, therefore, may arise as the result of the prohibited degrees, for example between a man and his step-daughter, where the only alternative would be to seek permission to marry by way of private Act of Parliament which is a lengthy, costly and by no means guaranteed method. Such cases are rare but not unknown (see, for example the Edward Berry and Doris Eileen Ward (Marriage Enabling) Act 1980).

In addition to the prohibited degrees of affinity, certain people cannot marry because of a blood relationship. They may cohabit, but in the case of these prohibited degrees of consanguinity, some relatives are prohibited also from having a sexual relationship, for example father and daughter, mother and son, brother and sister. A man or woman (provided in the case of a woman she is over 16) who knowingly has such a relationship, commits the criminal offence of incest (Sexual Offences Act 1956, ss. 10 and 11). Not all those within the prohibited degrees commit incest by having intercourse, for example, uncle and niece, even though they cannot marry.

There are many instances of members of a family living together in a relationship of companionship. Such relationships do not amount to cohabitation in the sense of a couple living together as husband and wife and will be described hereafter as family cohabitations. For certain purposes the law recognises such relationships where the test is not one of living together as husband and wife. Thus whilst the domestic violence legislation does not extend to family cohabitations (see *post*, p. 59) the principles of property law do so extend (see, for example, *Hussey* v. *Palmer* (1972), *post*, p. 18, in-laws; *Re Sharpe* (1980), *post*, p. 28, aunt and nephew) as does the Inheritance (Provision for Family and Dependants) Act 1975 (Chapter 5).

In addition to complying with the prohibited degrees of relationship two people are free to marry only if both are over the age of 16, both are unmarried, and one male and the other female (see Matrimonial Causes Act 1973, s. 11). Any marriage between two people not so qualified is void (*i.e.* non-existent), although their children may be treated as legitimate by means of the concept of the putative marriage (see *post*, p. 101). Any two people so disqualified may, however, be free to cohabit.

Sixteen is the minimum age for both parties to a marriage. If, however, either party is under the age of 18, the parents of the party under age must consent to the marriage (unless the person under age is a widow or widower). If the parents refuse to consent the parties wishing to marry may apply to the court for permission. A marriage without such consent, however, is legally valid. A couple, in such circumstances, may choose instead to live together and are free to do so provided their parents do not object. Parents have parental rights and duties (see Chapter 6) until the child is 18 and although the exercise and enforcement of these rights and duties diminishes as the child grows older, it is open to the parents to apply to the court to have the child made a ward of court and ask the court to direct that the couple shall not live together. As with all custody matters, in deciding the application the child's welfare is the first and paramount consideration (Guardianship of Minors Act 1971, s. 1). Alternatively there may be grounds for a person under the age of 17 being made subject to care proceedings under the Children and Young Persons Act 1969 (see Hoggett, *Parents and Children*, Chapter 5).

The possibility of care proceedings being taken is particularly likely if either party to a cohabitation is under the age of 16. It is a criminal offence for a boy over 14 or a man to have sexual intercourse with a girl under 16 (Sexual Offences Act 1956, s. 6). There is no corresponding offence where a girl or woman has sexual intercourse with a boy under 16, although she may be guilty of an indecent assault. In addition, it is a criminal offence to take a girl under 16 away from her parent or guardian against his will, even if there is no sexual motive (Sexual Offences Act 1956, s. 20).

Cohabitation involving children under 16 has been known to cause problems. One Social Services Department has been reported as saying that it would not accept or condone any situation where its officers might be involved in a case of intended or actual cohabitation by anyone under the age of 16.

Two people of the same sex cannot marry but can cohabit. Any purported marriage between two people manifestly of the same sex cannot even be termed a void marriage. If it were, the court would have power to make ancillary orders, for example, a maintenance order. A cohabitation between two people of the same sex may be one of companionship. If, however, there is a sexual relationship between two men sexual acts are only legal if both men are over 21, both consent and the act takes place in private (Sexual Offences Act 1967, s. 1).

This book is chiefly concerned with cohabitation between a man and a woman living together as husband and wife. Where the law recognises cohabitation it does so on the basis of relationships which essentially run parallel with marriage. It is only where the legal test is one other than of cohabitation, for example contribution to the home (see Chapter 2) that a party to a homosexual or lesbian relationship, like a party to a family cohabitation, may benefit.

CONSEQUENCES

The following chapters examine the legal recognition and consequences of cohabitation. They are concerned both with the mutual responsibilities of cohabitees and with those owed to and by third parties. It is necessary to consider not only the nature of the relationship, but also the purpose for which it is being claimed that a relationship exists. In view of the recognition that the law is giving to cohabitation the concluding chapter contains some thoughts on the future development of the legal treatment of cohabitees.

Further Reading

Bromley, *Family Law* (Butterworths, 5th ed.).
Cretney, *Principles of Family Law* (Sweet and Maxwell, 3rd ed.).
Eekelaar, *Family Law and Social Policy* (Weidenfeld and Nicolson).
Sweet and Maxwell's Family Law Statutes (2nd ed.).
Bradney, "The Family in Family Law" (1979) 9 Fam. Law 244.
Eekelaar, "The Place of Divorce in Family Law's New Role" (1975) 38 M.L.R. 241.
Hoggett, *Parents and Children* (Sweet and Maxwell).
Judicial Statistics.
Law Commission, *Reform of the Grounds of Divorce. The Field of Choice*, Cmnd. 3123.

Leete, "Changing Marital Composition," Population Trends 10.16.
Office of Population, Censuses and Surveys, "Population Trends."
Pearl, "The Legal Implications of a Relationship Outside Marriage"
   (1978) C.L.J. 252.
Samuels, "The Mistress and The Law" (1976) 6 Fam. Law 152.
Social Trends 9 (1979), Table 2.24.

2 The Home

Rights of ownership and occupation of the home are matters of considerable significance both during a relationship and, in particular, when a relationship—whether inside or outside marriage—breaks down. There are two main questions. First, who owns the home, and second, who is entitled to live in it?

HOME OWNERSHIP

The courts are increasingly willing to apply to questions of home ownership between the unmarried, the principles applicable between husband and wife during marriage (see, for example, *Cooke* v. *Head* (1972), *post*, p. 16). This represents a change from treating property disputes between cohabitees as ones between strangers and not by analogy to cases between husband and wife (see, for example, *Diwell* v. *Farnes* (1959)).

It has been said, however, that:

"... the rights of the parties to a marriage must be judged on the general principles applicable in any court of law when considering questions of title to property, and though the parties are husband and wife these questions of title must be decided by the principles of law applicable to the settlement of claims between those not so related, while making full allowances in view of that relationship."

(Lord Upjohn in *Pettit* v. *Pettit* (1969).)

Yet the courts have made very full allowances for that relationship and this is becoming so where there is a relationship outside marriage. One difference, of course, is that marriage is self-proving whereas cohabitation is not. Where a party to a cohabitation wishes to rely on the cohabitation as a basis for asserting a property right, it will be necessary to go into the detailed facts of the cohabitation. One influential factor is, for example, the parties' future intention to marry. In particular, recognition is given, for certain purposes, to an engagement, *i.e.* an agreement to marry. Until January 1, 1971 such agreements were governed generally by the law of contract and hence it was possible to sue for breach of promise to marry. Such actions were abolished by the Law Reform (Miscellaneous Provisions) Act 1970, s. 1. That Act made further provision with regard to property of engaged couples, so that on

11

termination of the engagement, the principles applicable to property acquired while the engagement was in force are those which apply between husband and wife (s. 2). The provisions relating to improvements to the home (see *post*, p. 19) and the procedural advantages of section 17 of the Married Women's Property Act 1882 also apply to people who have agreed to marry, but not to cohabitees who have not so agreed. It is certainly open to a cohabitee who has been living with another as husband and wife to argue that there was an engagement, but there may be difficulties of proof, particularly if it was an unannounced engagement.

In other respects it can be argued that the principles applicable between cohabitees should be the same whether or not there was an agreement to marry, *i.e.* the same principles as apply between spouses during marriage. There has been a tendency, however, for the courts to regard payments by a cohabitee towards the purchase of the home as a loan rather than a contribution entitling the contributor to a share in the property (see *post*, p. 18), and a reluctance to accept that a cohabitee has a share in the home owned by the other. In the case of spouses where a share in the home is established, there is a greater preparedness by the courts to decide on the basis of equality. It is suggested that in this respect the principles applicable between spouses should apply also between cohabitees.

Home ownership is determined on the basis of property rights and thus the question is who owns it, not who ought to own it. The starting point is therefore the title documents.

1. *Joint Names*

Where both cohabitees' names appear on the title documents, either as the registered proprietors in the case of registered land, or on the title deeds in the case of unregistered land, they are joint *legal* owners. Joint legal ownership does not tell the full story because of a rule of property law that joint legal owners prima facie own the home on trust for themselves as beneficiaries under the trust (Law of Property Act 1925, ss. 34 and 36). Ownership of the proceeds of sale depends upon the division of this *beneficial* ownership. The title documents should state, therefore, the ownership of the "beneficial interest" in the home, so as to make it clear how the proceeds of sale are to be divided. If it is intended that the parties should have equal shares, the title document should state that they hold the property upon trust for themselves as "joint tenants beneficially." If joint beneficial interests are spelt out in this way, it will be very difficult to show anything other than equal ownership of the proceeds of sale, for a declaration of the beneficial interests will usually be conclusive in the absence of fraud or mistake (*Leake* v. *Bruzzi* (1974)).

If the title document only states joint legal ownership and is silent as to beneficial ownership, it is open to either of the parties to argue that they intended that the beneficial interest in the home should be divided in unequal shares, in which case the parties hold the property on trust for themselves as "beneficial tenants in common" (see, for example, *W.* v. *W.* (1975)).

In *Crisp* v. *Mullings* (1976), Mrs. Crisp and Mr. Mullings lived together as husband and wife. They were joint legal owners of the home which was bought with the aid of a mortgage in their joint names and a deposit paid by Mr. Mullings. He paid the mortgage instalments on the basis that she would pay for food and other outgoings. They separated after two years and Mrs. Crisp sought an order that the property be sold and the proceeds divided equally. The title documents did not identify the beneficial interests and Mr. Mullings argued that as he had provided the deposit and paid the mortgage instalments, they held the home on "resulting trust" (see below) in his favour so he was solely entitled to the beneifcal ownership. The Court of Appeal rejected his argument and held that the joint legal ownership prima facie meant joint beneficial interests (a "joint tenancy") and thus equal shares, but on the facts, the ownership was subject to an adjustment to give Mr. Mullings additional benefit for the payment of :he deposit. A mathematical calculation had to be made to reflect this benefit, rather than award half each. There was thus a proportionate beneficial tenancy in common. They were entitled to share in the proceeds of sale in the proportions in which they had contributed to the purchase (see also *Lawrence* v. *McFarlane* (1976)).

Where the parties own the property jointly upon trust for themselves as "joint tenants beneficially" (hereafter "joint tenants"), they are both regarded as owning the whole interest. Should either of the joint tenants die, the whole interest passes automatically to the survivor, subject to the power of the court to order that the deceased's share be treated as part of his estate so as to meet claims under the Inheritance (Provision for Family and Dependants) Act 1975 (see Chapter 5). If it is intended that the parties should own distinct shares, then the home must be conveyed to them jointly upon trust for themselves as beneficial "tenants in common." On death of a tenant in common, his share does not pass to the survivor, but passes in accordance with the deceased's will or intestacy (see Chapter 5).

A beneficial joint tenancy may be severed by either of the joint tenants, thereby converting it into a tenancy in common. Severance can be achieved in any of the following ways: by giving written notice to the other joint tenant (Law of Property Act 1925, s. 36 (2)); by agreement

(*Burgess* v. *Rawnsley* (1975)); by one joint tenant dealing with his own beneficial share, for example, by way of sale or mortgage; or by a course of dealing between the joint tenants showing an intention that the property should be held in common and not jointly. Severance cannot be effected by will.

Ownership as joint tenants is the more usual arrangement, certainly amongst married couples, but may not suit the needs of all couples, as in the case of cohabitees who wish to own separate shares. The matter is one upon which legal advice should be taken at the time of the purchase of the home, so that the parties' intention can be clearly spelt out in the title documents.

2. *Sole Name*

If cohabitees intend that they should jointly own the home, then they should ensure that the property is conveyed to them jointly. Where the home is in the name of one of them only (usually the man), then that person is the sole legal owner and prima facie the other party will have no share in the property.

In the case of married partners, the court can reallocate matrimonial resources on divorce, notwithstanding property rights (Matrimonial Causes Act 1973, s. 24, see *post*, p. 130). A spouse has been given increased protection in recent years so that the contributions made by each of the parties to the welfare of the family, including any contribution made by looking after the home or caring for the family, are taken into account on divorce, when the court decides how to exercise its powers in relation to property adjustment orders (Matrimonial Causes Act 1973, ss. 24 and 25). The law acknowledges that, in the words of Sir Jocelyn Simon, "the cock can feather the nest because he does not have to spend most of his time sitting on it." The same acknowledgement does not apply between unmarried couples, whose rights are determined according to strict property principles; there is no power to order a property transfer on breakdown of the relationship (*Re Evers's Trust* (1980)).

It may be possible for a cohabitee (usually the woman), whose name is not on the title documents, to establish that she has a beneficial interest in the home by showing that the other cohabitee, as legal owner, holds the property on trust for them both (see Arden, *Housing: Security and Rent Control*, pp. 167–168).

Establishing a trust

As a general rule a cohabitee who is claiming a beneficial interest must show that it was the parties' common intention that she should have a beneficial interest in the home and that she has contributed towards its purchase.

(i) *Intention.* The court seeks to determine the parties' intention from their conduct, on the basis that the claimant can only acquire an interest on the strength of their intention at the time of acquisition of the home, not at any subsequent time. This may give rise to a fiction. When a couple buy a home, its ultimate division is unlikely to be contemplated. In determining the parties' intention, there is an element of artificiality. If the parties have made an agreement to cover the eventuality, this will go some way to showing their intention, unless the agreement is regarded as a "cohabitation contract," in which case it may be void as contrary to public policy, or unenforceable as not intended to give rise to a legal relationship (see Chapter 8). The decided cases on trusts between cohabitees have not been argued on such grounds and it seems that such agreements will be given effect. The legal owner can therefore declare a trust for the other cohabitee, stating that the property is to be held on trust for them both and setting out their respective shares and the intended use. (For a form of such a declaration see Moon (1978).) The declaration can be quite simple in form, but must be evidenced in writing and signed by the creator of the trust (Law of Property Act 1925, s. 53 (1) (*b*)). It is always best to seek legal advice on the drawing up of such an agreement so as to protect fully the parties' interests.

In the absence of any express agreement, the courts resort to the imputed common intention. Where the home is conveyed to a person other than the one who provided the purchase money, there is a general rule that beneficial ownership "results" to the one providing the purchase money. This rule is known as the "presumption of resulting trust." If, for example, one cohabitee provides the purchase money and the home is conveyed into the name of the other cohabitee, the latter, theoretically, holds the property on trust for the former. Similarly in the case of a wife providing the purchase money where the house is conveyed to the husband, he owns the legal estate subject to a resulting trust for the wife.

A special rule applies, however, where the home is purchased by a husband and conveyed to his wife. This is presumed to be a gift to her and the "presumption of advancement" applies, so that the wife owns the legal estate and the beneficial interest. The presumption of advancement does not apply between the unmarried (*Soar* v. *Foster* (1858)).

The presumptions of resulting trust and advancement are rebuttable by other evidence. In recent years the courts have paid little attention to the presumptions, especially the presumption of advancement which is now very doubtful, and have relied more on the conduct of the parties, particularly where both parties have contributed towards the acquisition of the home.

(ii) *Contribution*. A direct financial contribution to the purchase price will normally suffice to show that the legal owner should hold the home on trust for himself and the cohabitee making the contribution in the absence of evidence to the contrary, for example, evidence that the contribution was a loan or a gift. The resulting trust principle applies and the parties will have proportionate beneficial interests equivalent to their contribution. Thus if A contributes two-thirds of the purchase price and B one-third and the legal estate is vested in A, he will hold the home on trust for himself as to two-thirds and on trust for B as to one-third.

Mortgage repayments will count as contributions towards the purchase price; so in *Diwell* v. *Farnes* (1959), a woman who lived with a man as his wife but who was not married to him, was held entitled to a share, by way of resulting trust, in the proceeds of sale of the home owned by him, since her payments towards the repayment of the mortgage were contributions towards the purchase price of the home. Her share was in proportion to her contributions. In such a case, the amount of the share will be more difficult to calculate than a cash contribution to the purchase price.

A direct contribution by labour towards the acquisition of the home may also suffice to give a beneficial interest in the home. Thus in *Cooke* v. *Head* (1972), Miss Cooke and Mr. Head, a married man, decided to acquire land and build a bungalow on it. He paid a deposit of £390 and raised £3,000 on mortgage. The conveyance was taken in his name. Miss Cooke contributed nothing in cash, but helped by doing a lot of heavy work. She used a sledgehammer to demolish old buildings, worked a cement mixer, filled a wheelbarrow with rubble and helped with the painting. When the bungalow was nearly completed, they separated and Miss Cooke brought an action claiming the property was jointly owned. The Court of Appeal held that the principles which apply where spouses by their joint efforts acquired property for their joint use, apply also to an unmarried couple who acquire property by their joint efforts with the intention of setting up home together. Mr. Head therefore held the property on trust for himself and Miss Cooke, who, in all the circumstances, was awarded one-third of the proceeds of sale. In the words of Lord Denning:

> ". . . whenever two parties by their joint efforts acquire property to be used for their joint benefit, the courts may impose or impute a constructive or resulting trust. The legal owner is bound to hold the property on trust for them both. . . . It applies to husband and

wife, to engaged couples, and to man and mistress, and maybe to other relationships too."

The principle applies whether the couple build the home or renovate it. So in *Eves* v. *Eves* (1975), Mr. and Mrs. Eves were cohabitees and she was the mother of his children. They planned to marry when they were free to do so. They bought a house in a dilapidated condition and it was conveyed into Mr. Eves' sole name, after he had told Mrs. Eves that as she was under 21 the house could not be in joint names. He assured her it was to provide a home for themselves and their children. In fact he always intended that the home was to be in his name alone. Mr. Eves provided the purchase price, partly by cash and the balance on mortgage, and Mrs. Eves did a great deal of work to the house and garden. She stripped wallpaper, painted woodwork and brickwork, broke up concrete using a sledgehammer and carried the pieces to a skip, prepared the front garden for turfing and helped Mr. Eves demolish a shed and put up a new one. Mr. Eves then formed a relationship with another woman. Mrs. Eves obtained affiliation orders for the two children, but he paid little maintenance under the orders and soon fell into arrears. After various threats of violence, Mrs. Eves left the home and claimed that Mr. Eves held the house on trust for them both. It was decided by the Court of Appeal that he held the house on trust for himself and Mrs. Eves as to three-quarters for himself and one-quarter for her. Lord Denning, applying the principle in *Cooke* v. *Head*, held that, in view of Mr. Eves' behaviour in telling her that the house was to be their joint home and that it would have been conveyed into their joint names but for her age, it would be "inequitable" to deny her a share in the house. The other two judges found in her favour, on the basis that there was an implied agreement between the parties that she should contribute her labour towards the house in return for a share in the beneficial interest. The judges were therefore saying different things. Lord Denning's finding was irrespective of the parties' intention. He said that the trust arose not because that was the parties' intention, but because that was the equitable result (a constructive trust). The other two judges said that the law could infer a trust because that is what the parties had intended (an implied trust). The concept of the constructive trust is wider, and more uncertain, than that of the implied trust.

It is therefore possible to establish a beneficial interest on the basis of one of three types of trust: resulting, constructive and implied. They are not easy to distinguish; indeed the courts frequently do not distinguish them (see, for example, Lord Diplock in *Gissing* v. *Gissing* (1970) and Lord Denning in *Hussey* v. *Palmer* (1972)). Unlike a declaration of trust, any such trust need not be in writing (Law of Property Act 1925, s. 53 (2)). On Lord Denning's interpretation, the courts can take into account looking after the other cohabitee and caring for the children in determining the contribution made. In *Eves* v. *Eves* the children were an important consideration, in that Mrs. Eves' share was regarded as more in the nature of provision for the children than for her. Thus the court decided that the property need not be sold, provided that Mr. Eves paid the affiliation orders and also a reasonable amount off the arrears.

A further example of Lord Denning's use of the constructive trust is given in *Hussey* v. *Palmer* (1972), in a case concerning a family cohabitation. Mrs. Hussey went to live with her daughter and son-in-law, Mr. and Mrs. Palmer. The house, which was owned by Mr. Palmer, was too small for them all, so Mrs. Hussey paid £607 for an extension to be built. She then fell out with her daughter and son-in-law and left. She claimed a trust in her favour, a view which was accepted by two of the three judges in the Court of Appeal, on the principle that where it was inequitable on the grounds of justice and good conscience that the legal owner of property should take the property for himself and exclude another from it, the law would impute or impose a trust for the other's benefit. Mrs. Hussey had an interest in the house proportionate to the £607 which she paid.

To attribute a beneficial interest to people in the place of Miss Cooke, Mrs. Eves and Mrs. Hussey, raises problems with regard to the sale or mortgage of the property (see *post*, p. 23) and with regard to the rights of third parties; rights which the law is also anxious to protect. It is not surprising, therefore, that the courts have sometimes shown reluctance in finding that the claimant is entitled to a beneficial interest.

In *Richards* v. *Dove* (1974), an unmarried couple bought a house which was conveyed into the man's name. The house cost £3,500, of which Mr. Dove provided £350 and Miss Richards provided £150, the balance being obtained by mortgage granted to Mr. Dove. He paid the household bills and she paid for food and gas. The relationship broke up and Miss Richards claimed that Mr. Dove held the property on trust for them both. Her claim failed. The judge held that although the trust concept applies to cohabitees as well as spouses, there is a difference in the application of the concept, because a husband is under a legal duty to maintain his wife, whereas no such obligation arises as a result of cohabitation. A cohabitee must, therefore, show that the home has been acquired by their joint efforts and that her contribution was made with the intention of helping with the purchase of the home, and thus with the aim of acquiring some interest in the property. The judge held that Miss Richards had lent the money and could not have intended to acquire an interest in the home, and her contributions to the household expenses could not be regarded as giving her any interest in the home. She was, of course, entitled to have her loan repaid, but did not get the benefit of an interest in the home, which would have increased proportionately with the increase in value of the property. On breakdown of cohabitation where the home is in the man's sole name, it is clearly to his advantage to argue that any contribution made by the woman was only by way of loan. The argument applies equally to family cohabitations.

One of the arguments in *Richards* v. *Dove* was that the court should take into account not only direct contributions towards the acquisition of the home, but also indirect contributions, *i.e.* contributions such as to relieve the other party from paying sums which he would otherwise have had to pay. Such contributions must, it seems, be substantial and must be financial. The principle applicable in the case of the matrimonial home, which arguably extends to cohabitees, is that there is no distinction to be drawn between direct and indirect contributions, although in the latter case the relevant share in the beneficial interest is likely to be harder to calculate (*Gissing* v. *Gissing* (1970)).

It does appear, however, that indirect contributions must be made with the intention of helping towards the purchase of the home, and that it is not enough merely to contribute towards household expenses or to do the housekeeping. Thus, for example, a contribution towards rent has been held not to create a beneficial interest in favour of the contributor (*Diwell* v. *Farnes* (1959), *Savage* v. *Dunningham* (1973)).

The law is by no means certain, however, and the result depends upon whether the court approaches the matter on principles of property law as outlined above (see, for example, *Cowcher* v. *Cowcher* (1972)), in which case it is necessary to establish that the parties agreed that they should both have a share of the home, even if this can only be implied from their conduct by way of contribution, or on principles of reaching the "equitable" result, *i.e.* the result which is fair or just in all the circumstances.

Special mention must be made of contributions by way of improvements to the home. Where a husband or wife makes such a contribution he, or she, subject to any agreement between them to the contrary, is treated as having acquired a beneficial interest in the home, provided that the contribution is of a substantial nature and is in money or money's worth (Matrimonial Proceedings and Property Act 1970, s. 37). This provision does not apply to cohabitees who must rely on the trust concept and, as we have seen, the law is uncertain. The cases of *Cooke* v. *Head*, *Eves* v. *Eves* and *Hussey* v. *Palmer* suggest that such improvements can give a cohabitee a beneficial interest, but these cases conflict with suggestions in the House of Lords decision in *Pettit* v. *Pettit* (1969), and the matter is open to doubt. Section 37 has dispelled this doubt in relation to improvements made by spouses and engaged couples whose engagement is terminated (Law Reform (Miscellaneous

Provisions) Act 1970, s. 2 (1))). Section 37 does not, however, apply to cohabitees.

To succeed in establishing a contribution on the basis of improvements, the contribution must be substantial, in the words of Lord Denning in relation to Miss Cooke, "Much more than most women would do." Any such test is by its nature uncertain and makes it difficult for anyone, such as a social worker, to advise parties. The uncertainty of the law means many cases are contested, with the result that neither side wins, because the value of what is being fought over is lost in legal costs. In *Cooke* v. *Head*, the proceeds of sale were £2,546 of which Miss Cooke was awarded one-third (£849) and Mr. Head two-thirds (£1,697), but after costs Miss Cooke received about £705 and Mr. Head £98 (see *Cooke* v. *Head (No. 2)* 1974)). As Lord Denning said:

> "This shows that when the sole asset is the proceeds of a house, it is
> much better for the disputing parties to settle at the outset;
> because, if they go to law, much of the proceeds will be eaten up in
> law costs, even though the parties are both legally aided with a nil
> contribution."

(iii) *Quantifying the beneficial interest.* It is thus very difficult for those to whom cohabitees turn for advice, for example social workers, to advise, with any degree of certainty, people in the situation of Miss Cooke, Mrs. Eves and the like. There is the difficulty of establishing whether or not a sufficient contribution has been made and, if it has, the effect to be given to it. There is no formula for calculating the contributor's share of the beneficial interest. The amount of any financial contribution will be relevant, but each party's share of the beneficial interest does not depend solely on the monetary contributions each has made towards the acquisition of the home.

The cases are looked at broadly and the value of each party's share is determined as at the time when the parties separated, in the light of all the circumstances of the particular case. Thus Miss Cooke received a one-third share, the court adopting an approach similar to that on divorce (see *post*, p. 129), whereas Mrs. Eves received a quarter. Their rewards, however, do not compare with that given to Mrs. Turner in a case based on estoppel.

Estoppel

As an alternative to a claim based on a trust, it may be possible to argue that the legal owner has led the claimant to change his, or more usually her, position so that the owner is prevented (or "estopped") from denying the claimant's right to an interest in the home. The consequences can be even more rewarding to the claimant, to the extent of acquiring the whole property, at least for a time. Such was the case in *Pascoe* v. *Turner* (1979). Mrs. Turner moved into Mr. Pascoe's house as his housekeeper. They subsequently lived as man and wife. Some years later Mr. Pascoe left to live with another woman, but told Mrs. Turner "the house is yours and everything in it." The house was never conveyed to her. Mrs. Turner, with Mr. Pascoe's knowledge and encouragement, spent £230 on repairs and improvements. After a quarrel Mr. Pascoe claimed possession of the house. Mrs. Turner argued that the house was held on trust for her or, in the alternative, she had a licence to occupy the house for her lifetime.

The Court of Appeal decided that there was nothing on the facts from which an inference of a constructive trust could be drawn, but invoked the doctrine of estoppel, having regard to the way in which she had changed her position for the worse by spending money on the house, with the acquiescence and encouragement of Mr. Pascoe. He was required by the court to give effect to his promise and transfer the house outright to Mrs. Turner. The case is significant for the generosity with which Mrs. Turner's claim was treated. Her contribution to the acquisition of the home was far less than that of Miss Cooke or Mrs. Eves and hence no trust was held to exist, yet her reward was far greater. Indeed, she could not have hoped for more had she been married to Mr. Pascoe. The case is the closest yet to the court's wide powers to make property transfer orders on divorce (Matrimonial Causes Act 1973, s. 24, see *post*, p. 130).

Although the case is a useful guide for those, such as social workers, involved with advising claimants in the position of Mrs. Turner, it must be regarded with caution. One swallow does not make a summer and the generosity extended to Mrs. Turner cannot yet be accepted as the norm. A more usual remedy in a case where it is not possible to establish a trust, is for the claimant to have a life interest in the home (see, for example, *Greasley* v. *Cooke* (1980)), or a licence to occupy the home (see *post*, p. 26).

3. *Contents of the Home*

The principles applicable to ownership of the home generally apply also to the contents. The first question, therefore, is who paid for them? This may not be easy to prove, especially as, unlike the home, there may not be documents of title which can provide a starting point.

Moreover, on divorce the court has extensive discretionary powers over "family assets," a term used to describe things acquired by one or other of the parties to a marriage for the use of them and their children, but these powers are not available between cohabitees, whose rights are decided on principles of property law. The special rules applicable to ownership of money, for example, savings and joint bank accounts, are considered in Chapter 3. It should also be noted that the courts' protective powers under the domestic violence legislation, which will be considered in Chapter 4, extend to the home but not its contents.

Property belonging to each at the start of the cohabitation, and personal items acquired during cohabitation, will remain the property of each, as will personal gifts between the parties.

If there has been an engagement which has been terminated, ownership of gifts given by the parties to one another depends upon whether or not they were given conditionally upon the wedding taking place. If they were, they must be returned to the donor, but not otherwise, regardless of which party broke off the engagement (Law Reform (Miscellaneous Provisions) Act 1970, s. 3 (1)). An engagement ring does not normally have to be returned, even if the woman changes her mind. It is presumed to be an absolute gift, unless the man can prove that the ring was given on condition that it should be returned if the marriage did not take place (s. 3 (2)). As with other gifts, proving that it was conditional will not be easy. If the man makes it expressly conditional when slipping the ring on her finger, he is likely to get it back more quickly than he expected. The condition can be implied as, for example, where the ring is a family heirloom.

Engagement presents from other people, like wedding presents, are presumed to be given conditionally on the wedding taking place. If the wedding is called off, for whatever reason, the gifts should be returned to the donors.

As with all disputes between a couple on breakdown of their relationship, the matter should be resolved, if at all possible, between those involved, if necessary with legal advice, but without recourse to litigation. This is particularly so with regard to the contents of the home, for their value will soon disappear in legal costs, in which case no one benefits, except perhaps the legal advisers.

HOME OCCUPATION

Having considered the question of ownership of the home and its contents, the second question is who is entitled to live in it? The answer to the second question is dependent, in part, upon the answer to the first.

Where legal ownership of the home is in both parties jointly, they both have a right to live in the home by virtue of that joint ownership. Neither party can exclude the other unless an exclusion injunction is obtained from the court (see Chapter 4). Of particular importance is the need for both parties to join in any sale of the house. Both their names are on the title documents, therefore both signatures are needed for any transfer (Law of Property Act 1925, ss. 2 (2) and 27 (2)). If they cannot agree on a sale of the property, either of them can apply to the court under section 30 of the Law of Property Act 1925, for an order that the property be sold and the proceeds of sale be divided. The matter is at the court's discretion. The court will normally order a sale if the purpose for which the house was bought, for example, cohabitation, has come to an end. The court will consider the needs of any children and, if the house is still needed to provide them with a home, the court might not order a sale until a later date (see *Re Evers's Trust* (1980)). Such a decision will favour the party with custody, who will usually be the children's mother (see *post*, p. 104), but there is no guarantee of success (see, for example, *Burke* v. *Burke* (1974)).

Where the home is legally owned by only one party (usually the man) he prima facie has the sole right to live in the home. If the other party can establish that she has a beneficial interest in the home, that interest gives her a right to live in the home. She is at a disadvantage, however, compared with a cohabitee whose name appears on the title documents, for her interest will not be there for all the world to see. On the face of the title documents, there is nothing to prevent the legal owner disposing of the home, either by way of sale or mortgage, for the purchaser (*i.e.* buyer) or mortgagee (*i.e.* lender) will not know of the beneficial interest. Is there anything the other party can or need do to protect her beneficial interest?

1. *Protecting Rights Arising from a Beneficial Interest*

Where a person (the beneficiary) has a beneficial interest in a home owned by someone else (the owner), the home is subject to a "trust for sale." This raises conveyancing problems so far as any dealings with the home by the owner are concerned, for example, by way of sale or mortgage.

As the home is held on trust for sale, the beneficiary can protect her interest in the proceeds of sale by seeking the appointment of herself (if adult) as second trustee of the trust for sale. Any purchaser of the home who pays the purchase money over to the two trustees, acquires the home free from the beneficial interests, which are said to be "overreached" (Law of Property Act 1925, ss. 2 and 27).

The problem is, of course, that people in this position will not appreciate the subtleties of conveyancing law. Is there any other way, therefore, of protecting the beneficial interest whether or not there is a sale of the property?

The method of protection will depend upon whether the home is registered or unregistered land. Registered land means land the ownership of which is registered at the Land Registry under the Land Registration Acts, thereby providing a single title guaranteed by the State, in place of the traditional system of unregistered land, proof of ownership of which depends upon production of title deeds. The system of registration of title only operates in certain parts of the country, but is being extended progressively to all parts.

Where the home is registered land, the beneficial interest may be protected by the entry on the register of "a caution" (Land Registration Act 1925, ss. 54, 101 (3); *Elias* v. *Mitchell* (1972)). The interest then becomes a protected minor interest which is binding on any purchaser or mortgagee. Any purchaser should then pay the purchase price to two trustees so as to overreach the beneficial interest (Law of Property Act 1925, ss. 2 and 27). The beneficiary will also have notice of any disposal and can then, if necessary, seek an injunction to prevent the transaction (*Waller* v. *Waller* (1967)).

If the interest is not protected as a minor interest by registration of a caution, it may nevertheless be an "overriding interest" if the beneficiary is in "actual occupation" of the home. The list of overriding interests is contained in section 70 of the Land Registration Act 1925, and the relevant paragraph is section 70 (1) (*g*):

"The rights of every person in actual occupation of the land or in receipt of the rents and profits thereof, save where enquiry is made of such person and the rights are not disclosed."

It is not the occupation which is binding, but the rights arising under the beneficial interest which are binding because of the occupation. The interest is "overriding" because any purchaser or mortgagee takes the property subject to that interest even though it is not registered, for an interest can only be an overriding interest if it is not protected as a minor interest by registration (Land Registration Act 1925, s. 3 (xvi)).

In *Williams and Glyn's Bank Ltd.* v. *Boland* (1980), a husband bought the home with a substantial contribution from his wife, but he was registered as sole owner. The wife had a beneficial interest by virtue of her contribution. In order to raise money for his business, the husband later mortgaged the house to the Bank without his wife's knowledge. His business failed and the Bank sought possession. The question was whether or not the wife's beneficial interest took priority over the Bank's mortgage. The House of Lords held that it did. A spouse who buys the home with the help of a contribution from the other spouse, holds the home, and not merely the proceeds of sale, on trust for them both. The trust confers a right which is binding as an overriding interest because the contributor is in actual occupation. The overriding interest entitles the contributor (in this case Mrs. Boland) to remain in possession. The result is that any purchaser or lender ought to make enquiries of every person in actual occupation. If an occupier discloses any interest, the purchaser or lender takes subject to the interest, unless he obtains a "release" from the occupier, for example, by getting the occupier to join in the conveyance or mortgage, otherwise it is only where enquiry is made of such person and the rights are not disclosed that the purchaser or lender takes free from any interest.

Whether a person is in actual occupation or not is to be decided according to the ordinary meaning of the term. Certainly a wife who is physically present and living in the home is in actual occupation, and the same, it seems, applies between cohabitees. In *Hodgson* v. *Marks* (1971), the Court of Appeal decided that a purchaser must pay heed to anyone occupying the home. In *Williams and Glyn's Bank Ltd.* v. *Boland* the case of cohabitees was considered and the suggested solution was to read section 70 (1) (*g*) for what it said, so that anyone in occupation who had rights in the home was entitled to have those rights protected, so long as they were in occupation. Personal rights, for example those of a lodger, are not protected, but rights arising from a beneficial interest are protected, whether the beneficiary is a wife, a cohabitee, a mistress or whatever. Parties to a family cohabitation or homosexual cohabitation, with a beneficial interest, will thus qualify. The need to make enquiries of occupiers as to their rights could, of course, be embarrassing for potential purchasers and mortgagees.

Where the home is unregistered land (see *ante*, p. 24), protection of the beneficial interest depends upon any purchaser or mortgagee having prior notice of the interest, for which purpose the beneficial interest should be endorsed on the title deeds. It is not clear whether or not the interest is capable of registration as a land charge, *i.e.* a charge on the owner's interest which is binding on anyone who buys or lends money on the security of the house. The authorities do not support such registration (see *Re Rayleigh Weir Stadium* (1954) and also Land Charges Act 1972, s. 2 (4) (iii) (*b*)). There is nothing to be lost, other than the risk of the costs involved, in registering the interest as a "Class C (iii)" land charge (*i.e.* a general equitable charge), for even if it is later ordered to be cleared from the register, it will have given any purchaser or mortgagee notice of the beneficial interest and any purchaser should then pay the purchase money to two trustees (Law of Property Act 1925, ss. 2 and 27). If necessary, the beneficiary can seek an injunction to restrain any dealing with the home.

Even if the beneficial interest is neither endorsed on the deeds nor registered, it may nevertheless be protected. The decision in *Williams and Glyn's Bank Ltd.* v. *Boland*, although a case on registered land, suggests that a purchaser or mortgagee of unregistered land will be regarded as having notice of the beneficial interest of anyone living in the house. There have been earlier statements to the contrary, as in *Caunce* v. *Caunce* (1969), where it was held that a bank to whom the house was mortgaged was not to be regarded as having notice of the wife's beneficial interest merely because she was living in the home, together with her husband. Such statements, however, are out of line with subsequent decisions, and it is doubted that they have survived the *Boland* case (see, for example, Lord Scarman's comments in that case).

2. *Licence*

Where a cohabitee's name is not on the title documents and she has no beneficial interest in the home, she cannot seek to rely on the cohabitation to give her a right of occupation. Marriage confers on the parties a duty to cohabit and a duty to support. A wife has a right, arising from the marriage, to be provided with a home. A spouse with no legal title to the home (whether or not he or she has a beneficial interest) has a statutory right of occupation (Matrimonial Homes Act 1967, s. 1). This right is a "charge" on the interest of the owning spouse and can be protected by either registering a Class F land charge if the home is unregistered land, or by registering a notice or caution if the home is registered land (the right cannot be an overriding interest) (1967 Act, s. 2). Once the right of occupation is registered, it is binding on third parties, so, for example, anyone who buys a house which has such a charge registered against it, will buy it subject to the spouse's right to remain there.

A cohabitee has no right of occupation under the Matrimonial Homes Act 1967 and, in the absence of any beneficial interest, will only be able to establish a right to live in the home if he or she has a licence to do so, otherwise the owner is free to sell the home with vacant possession. In *Tanner* v. *Tanner* (1975), Mr. Tanner, a married man, was the father of twins born to a single woman ("Mrs. Tanner") who took his name. He provided a house for her and the children and she gave up the tenancy of a rent-controlled flat. He made it clear to her, however, that he did not intend to marry her. The house was in his name and he provided the purchase price by way of mortgage. Mr. Tanner later divorced his wife and married another woman. He wanted to evict "Mrs. Tanner" and the twins so that he could occupy the house with his new wife. The Court of Appeal decided that "Mrs. Tanner" had made no contribution from which it could be inferred that she was to have any beneficial interest, but there was an agreement between the parties under which she had a contractual licence to live in the house with the children so long as they were of school age and required the accommodation. She had given good consideration (see below) for the licence by giving up her rent-controlled flat and looking after the children. As she and the children had been rehoused by the local authority, she was not seeking to reoccupy the house and it was thus no longer practicable to enforce the licence. Had it been so, the court could have issued an injunction restraining Mr. Tanner from revoking the licence and thus preventing him from selling the house. Instead, "Mrs. Tanner" was awarded compensation of £2,000 for loss of the licence.

Establishing a licence

Cohabitation itself is insufficient to confer rights of occupation. In order that the licence cannot be revoked at the wish of the owner on giving reasonable notice (a bare licence), the claimant must show that the parties have entered into a contract by which one party has agreed, for consideration (*i.e.* something in return), that the other shall have a right to occupy the home. The agreement may be express or implied. In either case there must be a meeting of the minds of the parties, clear terms of agreement, an intention to create a legal relationship and consideration. In "Mrs. Tanner's" case, the consideration was giving up her flat and looking after the children. It is questionable whether or not the mother's looking after the children was consideration in itself, because she was under an existing duty to do so (see Chapter 6, but see also *Ward* v. *Byham* (1956)).

The case of *Tanner* can be contrasted with that of *Horrocks* v. *Forray* (1976). A married man, who lived with his wife, kept a mistress (Mrs. Forray) for 17 years before his death. They had a daughter and he bought a house for mother and daughter. The house was in his name, although he had contemplated transferring it to her or creating a trust for his daughter, but for tax reasons did neither. Only on his death did his wife discover the existence of the house and the mistress. His executors gave the mistress notice to quit so that the house could be sold with vacant possession, otherwise it was probable that the deceased's estate would be insolvent. In reply the mistress claimed a contractual licence. The case differed from that of "Mrs. Tanner" for there "consideration was perfectly clear" whereas that was not so in Mrs. Forray's case. In all the circumstances, there was no contractual licence and the widow's claim for possession was granted.

The law is again unclear as to precisely what must be established.

There is the impression that the courts are trying to achieve the equitable result in the particular case, thus in *Horrocks* v. *Forray* the court's sympathy was with the widow rather than the mistress, yet such reasoning leads to total uncertainty. There is a suggestion that arrangements made between two people living happily together are not intended to affect their legal relationship. In *Horrocks* v. *Forray* the fact that the man had provided well for his mistress and child was taken as not indicating a contract. This suggests, therefore, that a contract is less likely in a happy relationship (as in *Horrocks*), than one that is breaking down (as in *Tanner*)—but is this realistic?

The need to provide children of the union with a home is an influencing factor, but Lord Denning in *Tanner* suggested that the duty extends beyond the children:

"This man had a moral duty to provide for the babies of whom he was the father. I would go further. I think he had a legal duty towards them. Not only towards the babies. But also towards their mother."

The duty to the mother must, presumably, be as mother and not as cohabitee, for there is no duty to support a cohabitee. For such a duty to arise there has to be a contract under which the claimant has given consideration, for example, has suffered a detriment by moving into the home.

In *Re Sharpe* (1980), an aunt's loan to her nephew, on the common assumption that she was to have a right to occupy the home, meant that she had acted to her detriment and the court implied an irrevocable licence to occupy the house until the loan was repaid. Furthermore, the aunt's irrevocable licence was held to be not merely a contractual licence, but one which arose under a constructive trust and, as such, conferred on her an interest in the property (see *post*, p. 30).

There is the suggestion from recent cases that the courts may not insist on the need to prove an express or implied contract and may instead impose the equivalent of a contract. This form of licence has been referred to as an "equitable licence" (see, for example, Lord Denning in *Hardwick* v. *Johnson* (1978)). The majority of cases, however, support the need to find an agreement, express or implied.

One of the factors influencing the courts in finding a trust rather than a licence is the parties' intention to marry. This influenced the courts in favour of a trust for Miss Cooke and Mrs. Eves, whereas it was clear that Mr. Tanner never intended marriage with "Mrs. Tanner." This seems a somewhat artificial limitation. Surely what is important is their intentions with regard to the home, not their marital status? There is the impression that some judges regard an intention to marry as giving the relationship an air of respectability, justifying the award of a beneficial interest, which is not justified in cases of cohabitation with no plans of marriage. So, for example, the relationship in *Richards* v. *Dove* was seen as one of convenience, with no thought of marriage on the part of either party.

Also significant is the presence or absence of cohabitation. Mrs. Forray was a mistress, not a cohabitee (see Chapter 1). The relationship was not equivalent to that of husband and wife and the preparedness to extend to cohabitees the legal protection enjoyed by spouses has not been accorded so readily to mistresses.

Duration of a licence

If a licence can be established, there will be the question of how long does it last? "Mrs. Tanner's" licence was said to be one to occupy the home so long as the children were of school age. Such an order will not be appropriate in all cases however, and, in the absence of express agreement, the licence may be terminated on giving reasonable notice. In *Chandler* v. *Kerley* (1978), Mr. Chandler bought the house of his mistress, Mrs. Kerley, and her husband who were living apart. He paid substantially less than the asking price, on the understanding that Mrs. Kerley would continue to live in the house until she obtained a divorce and he joined her there. Six weeks after the purchase, the relationship between Mr. Chandler and Mrs. Kerley ended and he ordered her out of the house. The Court of Appeal decided that, although Mr. Chandler knew that Mrs. Kerley wanted the house as a home for her children as well as herself, it would be wrong to infer that he had assumed the burden of another man's wife and children. Mrs. Kerley's contractual licence was terminable on reasonable notice and 12 months' notice was reasonable. What constitutes reasonable notice must depend upon the circumstances of the case and in particular whether or not there are children in need of a home. Thus one week's notice is unlikely to be sufficient and, as a very minimum, a month seems more likely. If the owner ejects the licensee before the expiration of reasonable notice, the owner will be liable in damages for breach of contract. Once the licence has been terminated, an injunction can be sought to prevent re-entry by the licensee and, if necessary, to restrain violence (*Egan* v. *Egan* (1975)).

Effect on third parties

Rights arising under a contract cannot generally bind a person who is not a party to that contract. The effect of a contractual licence, however, is unclear. On principle, if the owner sells the home, the purchaser will not be bound by a contractual licence even if he has notice of the licence, because the licence does not create a property right. The position may be different, however, if the contractual licence can be said to give rise to an interest under a constructive trust, in which case the interest will be enforceable against a purchaser of the home, provided that the purchaser bought the home with notice of the licence (*Errington* v. *Errington* (1952), *Binions* v. *Evans* (1972)). The same would not be so if the purchaser had no notice of the licence, provided that he was a genuine purchaser.

It is suggested that the rights under a licence are personal rights in favour of the licensee, and not proprietary rights affecting the home. It is thus not possible to register a licence so as to give prospective purchasers and other third parties notice of the licence. There have been suggestions, however, that a licence can confer an interest in the property. In *Re Sharpe* (*ante*, p. 28) the nephew, owner of the property, went bankrupt and the judge decided that the aunt's irrevocable licence was not merely a contractual licence, but arose under a constructive trust and as such gave her an interest in the home which was binding on the trustee in bankruptcy, and so she was entitled to remain in the home until her loan was repaid. He so decided with hesitation, because of the very confused state of the law. His call for a full review of the law is worth stressing "in order to do justice to the many thousands of people who never come into court at all but who wish to know with certainty what their proprietary rights are...."

3. *Injunction*

Where a cohabitee is in need of protection for herself or her children from her partner, she may be entitled to an injunction under the Domestic Violence and Matrimonial Proceedings Act 1976, excluding him from the home (see Chapter 4). The courts' powers under the Act are irrespective of property rights (*Davis* v. *Johnson* (1978), *post*, p. 62), so a battered cohabitee with or without property rights in the home can apply for an injunction to exclude his or her partner, even if the party against whom the order is sought is the sole owner or sole tenant of the home. An injunction gives a right of occupation, usually for a temporary period, so as to enable the applicant to find other accommodation. In the words of Lord Scarman in *Davis* v. *Johnson*:

"I find nothing illogical or surprising in Parliament legislating to override a property right, if it be thought to be socially necessary. If in the result a partner with no property rights who obtains an injunction ... thereby obtains for the period of the injunction a right of occupation, so be it. It is no more than the continuance by court order of a right which previously she had by consent; and it will endure only for so long as the county court thinks necessary." The remedy is less extensive than the recommendation of the Select Committee on Violence in Marriage, that consideration be given to amending the guardianship legislation, so that on breakdown of cohabitation the court could permit the parent caring for the children to have sole occupation of the property during their minority, even if that parent had no legal interest in the property (para. 52).

4. *Mortgage Arrears*

Where a cohabitee has no legal or beneficial interest in the home owned by her partner and the partner defaults on his mortgage payments, the non-owner has no right to make the payments so as to prevent the mortgagee (*i.e.* the lender, usually a building society) taking proceedings for possession of the home, and no right to be given notice of such proceedings (*Hastings and Thanet Building Society* v. *Goddard* (1970)). It is advisable for the non-owner to see if the mortgagee will accept payment, but there is no obligation on the mortgagee to do so and he may well refuse to accept payment, because to accept might estop him from taking later possession proceedings. In such proceedings the non-owner should make it clear to the court that payment has been offered, and ask the court to adjourn the proceedings or postpone the possession order. The non-owner could not claim the benefit of the Administration of Justice Act 1970, s. 36 (as amended by the Administration of Justice Act 1973, s. 8) which gives the court power to adjourn the proceedings, stay or suspend execution of the possession order, or postpone the date for possession, because this power applies only where the mortgagor (*i.e.* the borrower) is likely to be able to pay all sums due within a reasonable time. A spouse, but not a cohabitee, has the right to pay mortgage arrears (Matrimonial Homes Act 1967, s. 1 (5)), thereby preventing the mortgagee from gaining possession of the home. Supplementary benefit may well be available for this purpose.

The issue could also arise in proceedings brought by a cohabitee under the Domestic Violence and Matrimonial Proceedings Act 1976 (see Chapter 4). Suppose the man is ordered out of the home owned by him and he defaults on his mortgage payments. In any possession proceedings by the mortgagee, it is suggested that the woman's right of occupation arising from the injunction ought to be good reason, during the continuance of the injunction, for postponement of the possession order, otherwise the injunction would be worthless. Notwithstanding that the Administration of Justice Act 1970, s. 36, is of no help because it only protects a mortgagor (*i.e.* the man as borrower), the court should at least adjourn proceedings to enable the woman to find alternative accommodation.

5. *Tenancies*

Where the home is rented by cohabitees rather than owned by them, their rights of occupation will depend upon the nature of the tenancy. If the tenancy is taken in their joint names, both of them will have the right to live in the home; one cannot exclude the other without a court order and both will be liable for all the obligations, for example, the rent.

If the joint tenancy is a "protected" tenancy (see Arden, *op. cit.*, Chapter 4) and one of the cohabitees leaves the home during the tenancy, the other will be regarded as the protected tenant so as to become the statutory tenant under the Rent Act at the end of the protected tenancy (*Lloyd* v. *Sadler* (1978)). In the case of a contractual tenancy, both tenants remain responsible under the tenancy for all the obligations and one cannot become sole tenant unless the landlord consents.

Where the tenancy is in the name of only one cohabitee, he is the tenant and the other cohabitee is merely a licensee. In the absence of any agreement, the licensee can be required to leave the home on being given reasonable notice by the tenant (see *ante*, p. 29).

If the statutory tenant leaves the home intending to return at some future time and leaves some indication in the home of that intention, his tenancy will continue. Leaving a cohabitee in occupation with an intention by the tenant to return, will be sufficient to continue the tenancy (*Brown* v. *Brash* (1948)). If the statutory tenant leaves the home with no intention of returning, the tenancy will not continue. A non-tenant cohabitee who is left in the home is not entitled to remain in possession. A wife, however, occupies the house on behalf of her husband so that he is regarded as continuing in possession despite his leaving with no intention to return, and the wife cannot be evicted except on the statutory grounds (*Brown* v. *Draper* (1944)). In *Colin Smith Music Ltd.* v. *Ridge* (1975), an unmarried couple lived together as man and wife in premises of which the man was statutory tenant. They had two children. The man later left and surrendered his tenancy and the landlords claimed possession. The Court of Appeal held that a cohabitee's position was not analogous to that of a wife and it could not be said that a woman who had borne the tenant's children, occupied the home on his behalf. She was therefore a mere licensee and the landlords were entitled to possession.

It is interesting to compare this situation with that on the death of a statutory tenant, in which event a surviving cohabitee may qualify as a member of the tenant's family and thus entitled to remain in possession (see Chapter 5).

A cohabitee has no right to pay the rent if her tenant partner defaults on his payments. A spouse has this right (Matrimonial Homes Act 1967, s. 1 (5)), and can thus prevent the landlord from gaining possession. Moreover, on granting a decree of divorce or decree of nullity, the court may transfer a protected or statutory tenancy from one spouse to the other (Matrimonial Homes Act 1967, s. 7). The courts have no such power on breakdown of cohabitation.

It is advisable for a non-tenant cohabitee to enquire of the landlord whether he is prepared to accept rent from her. He is under no obligation to do so, however, and may be reluctant, particularly if the man has left for good. The landlord may be prepared to grant her a tenancy in his place.

Where the tenancy is a council house, much will depend upon the particular authority's practice. There is a growing move away from granting tenancies of council houses to husbands alone, in favour of granting a joint tenancy to husband and wife. The practice is slowly being extended to cohabitees, although some authorities are reluctant so to extend it. Where there is a joint tenancy and the relationship breaks down, the woman should have a stronger claim to the home than if the tenancy is in the man's sole name (see Select Committee on Violence in Marriage, para. 50). Her claim to remain in the home is particularly strong if there are children of the relationship.

On breakdown of marriage, some authorities insist on the wife obtaining a custody order before transferring the tenancy into her name. Such an order is unnecessary, however, in the case of an illegitimate child, for the mother has sole custody (see Chapter 6). Her custody should therefore suffice to justify a transfer. Some authorities, however, are reluctant to transfer a tenancy unless there is a court order in the applicant's favour, for example, an affiliation order, on the basis that they are not justified in effecting a transfer in the absence of such an order. Moreover, to transfer the tenancy may prejudice any matrimonial proceedings, particularly as to custody, as to which adequate accommodation is an essential requirement. A cohabitee is at a disadvantage in this respect, compared with a spouse, for a cohabitee cannot take any form of matrimonial proceedings. A spouse has the advantage that in divorce proceedings a council tenancy is property within section 24 of the Matrimonial Causes Act 1973, so as to give the court power to order a transfer from one spouse to the other (see *Thompson* v. *Thompson* (1975), *Rodewald* v. *Rodewald* (1977)). Whether the court will exercise the power, or not, is another matter, particularly if the local authority objects to the transfer (*Regan* v. *Regan* (1977)). A cohabitee is limited to

seeking an injunction under the Domestic Violence and Matrimonial
Proceedings Act 1976 (see Chapter 4). The existence of such an injunction should certainly suffice for the transfer of the tenancy, indeed the
court itself has been known to effect a transfer (see *Spindlow* v. *Spindlow*
(1979), *post*, p. 65), but it is to be regretted if local authorities insist on a
cohabitee obtaining an injunction before transferring a tenancy, for if a
cohabitee has been forced out of the home, where is she to go in the
meanwhile, particularly if she has children?

If a cohabitee is successful in obtaining the transfer of a tenancy,
there may be a problem of rent arrears. Here the cohabitee is at a
disadvantage if the tenancy was originally a joint one, for joint tenancies mean joint responsibilities as well as joint rights, so the cohabitee in
whose favour the tenancy is transferred, remains liable for rent arrears
even if they are the fault of the other tenant. If the tenancy was
originally in the sole name of one cohabitee, for example the man, and
the tenancy is transferred to the other cohabitee, she is not responsible
for any rent arrears unless she incurs them herself. The authority may
refuse, however, to transfer the tenancy until payment of the arrears.
Such a practice is to be regretted because the transfer may be worthless
in face of the arrears. The authority should look to the original tenant
whose liability the arrears are.

REFORM

The proportion of married couples who buy their homes in joint names
has greatly increased in recent years. The majority of married couples
now own their home jointly. The advantages of such ownership have
already been discussed; in particular it limits problems over the division of the proceeds of sale. The Law Commission see joint ownership
as necessary to reflect the modern view of marriage as a partnership.
The Commission have proposed the introduction of a principle of
co-ownership of the matrimonial home (Law Com. No. 86) under
which, in the absence of agreement to the contrary, and certain other
exceptions, a matrimonial home would be owned equally between
husband and wife. The rights of cohabitees are not dealt with. The
principle is limited to married couples, thus parties to a void marriage
are also excluded.

The exclusion of cohabitees suggests that co-ownership is seen as a
matter of status arising from the marriage, rather than a matter of
contribution towards the marriage. Were it to be seen as a matter of
contribution, then it should apply to cohabitees, for they often contribute as much as spouses. It can be argued that it is not the entering of a
relationship that should be the test, but the fulfilment of it. Once a

contribution has been established, then, in the absence of agreement to the contrary, the fair division should be an equal one and the principle of co-ownership could then operate. The interests of the parties would arise, not as suggested by the Law Commission from the marriage relationship, but from the contribution to a relationship whether inside or outside marriage.

Reform of the law has not been concerned with the property rights of cohabitees, and none of the major property legislation extends to cohabitation. Innovation to date has rested with the judges through the concepts of the trust, the licence and estoppel. In the words of a Court of Appeal judge:

> "There is no ... body of legislation governing the distribution of the property, or the evaluation or adjustment of the proprietary rights, of two parties who have been living together as man and wife, have never been married and have parted company. To say that it would be difficult to devise such legislation would be an under-statement." (Stamp L.J., in *Cantliff* v. *Jenkins* (1978).)

Further Reading

Bromley, *Family Law* (Butterworths, 5th ed.).

Cretney, *Principles of Family Law* (Sweet and Maxwell, 3rd ed.).

Eekelaar, *Family Law and Social Policy* (Weidenfeld and Nicolson).

Sweet and Maxwell's Family Law Statutes (2nd ed.).

Arden, *Housing: Security and Rent Control* (Sweet and Maxwell).

Hoath, "Cohabitation and Property" (1976) Legal Action Group Bulletin 154.

Hoath, *Council Housing* (Sweet and Maxwell).

Law Commission, Third Report on Family Property (Law Com. No. 86).

Masson, "The Mistress's Limited Rights of Occupancy" (1979) Conv. 184.

Migdal, "An Equitable Affair?" (1979) 9 Fam. Law 195.

Moon, "The Rights of Cohabitees—1. The Home" (1978) Legal Action Group Bulletin 288.

Report from the Select Committee on Violence in Marriage. Session 1974–75, Vol. 1 (H.C. 553-i).

Richards, "The Mistress and the Family Home" (1976) Conv. 351.

Todd and Jones, "Matrimonial Property" (Office of Population, Censuses and Surveys, 1972).

3 Money

At some stage in every relationship, matters of money are important. To what extent do cohabitees retain financial independence? Cohabitees have been described as "strangers in law" (*Diwell* v. *Farnes* (1959)), a statement which is certainly true in relation to direct support obligations during the parties' lifetime. A contrast can be drawn between the lack of financial duty between cohabitees during their lifetime and the right to seek maintenance on death (see Chapter 5), thereby highlighting the different legal approaches to cohabitation, depending upon the context in which the relationship is discussed. Is it right that a cohabitee has no right against his or her partner during that partner's lifetime, yet can claim against the partner's estate when he dies? The distinction is justified by the Law Commission on the basis that the deceased may have been providing for the applicant and may have wished to continue so doing, but his will or the law of intestacy does not give effect to those wishes (Law Com. No. 61, para. 90). The distinction arises because any claim during a couple's lifetime has to be made under matrimonial law, which by its nature excludes the unmarried, whereas on death a claim is based on dependency, which can occur outside marriage. There does seem to be a lack of consistency in the legal approach to cohabitation (see Chapter 9).

This chapter is concerned with financial obligations between cohabitees during their lifetime; their financial obligations upon death are considered in Chapter 5 and their financial obligations to their children in Chapter 6.

MAINTENANCE

There is a general rule that spouses are under a duty to maintain each other. At common law this duty fell upon the husband alone, but recent legislation has made the duty reciprocal (see, for example, Matrimonial Causes Act 1973, ss. 23–25; Supplementary Benefits Act 1976, s. 17; Domestic Proceedings and Magistrates' Courts Act 1978, s. 1). The courts apply the duty on the principle that each spouse comes before the court on a basis of equality (*Calderbank* v. *Calderbank* (1975)).

Cohabitees are under no duty to maintain each other. English law recognises the duty to maintain and the right to be maintained as arising out of the marriage relationship, without such a relationship such rights and obligations do not arise. If parties to a cohabitation subsequently marry, can account be taken of the cohabitation when assessing marital obligations? In *Campbell* v. *Campbell* (1977), a couple lived together for three and a half years before marrying. The marriage lasted just two years. In divorce proceedings brought by Mrs. Campbell, she argued that the pre-marital cohabitation should be taken into account in determining the length of the marriage, as required by the Matrimonial Causes Act 1973 (s. 25 (1) (*d*)), when assessing maintenance. The judge rejected the argument on the basis that rights, duties and obligations begin on the marriage and not before, and pre-marital cohabitation cannot be taken as part of the marriage. The courts, however, have been prepared to take into account cohabitation after divorce (*Chaterjee* v. *Chaterjee* (1976)) and in some circumstances pre-marital cohabitation is relevant. In *Kokosinski* v. *Kokosinski* (1980), the parties lived together for only four months after their marriage, having cohabited for 25 years before marrying. The judge stressed that the court should not construe the legislation too narrowly. He held that section 25 of the Matrimonial Causes Act 1973 requires the court to have regard to the conduct of the parties and also to all the circumstances of the case, under both of which behaviour which occurs outside marriage can be taken into account, at least in a case where the conduct affected the finances of the other spouse. The court, it was said, could not do justice between the parties unless it took into account the wife's conduct during the 25 years that she and the husband had been cohabiting. She had been faithful, loving and hard-working and had helped to build up the family business, manage the home and bring up their son. The judge considered that a lump sum payment to her of £8,000 was appropriate. In so deciding, he expressed the perhaps too sanguine view that:

"... it will be said by some that to recognise the relationship which existed before marriage as relevant to financial redistribution, is to encourage relationships outside marriage. To them I would answer that the occasions on which a court is likely to feel that justice requires such recognition are likely to be few, possibly very few. It would, however, not be helpful to speculate on situations which may never arise. In my judgment, on the particular facts of the present case, my decision will do nothing to undermine the institution of marriage."

It is ironic that, had the parties not been married for the four months, the wife could have claimed nothing.

Can cohabitees impose a duty upon themselves by making a contract to maintain each other? Maintenance agreements between spouses are common and enforceable (Matrimonial Causes Act 1973, s. 34), but agreements between cohabitees are another matter (see Chapter 8). Their validity has never been upheld and there is the likelihood that a maintenance agreement between cohabitees would be considered contrary to public policy. This has been the view of the courts in the past, for example, it has been said that:

"... the law will not enforce an immoral promise, such as a promise between a man and a woman to live together without being married or to pay a sum of money or to give some other consideration in return for an immoral association." (Lord Wright in *Fender* v. *St. John Mildmay* (1937).)

It may be, however, that society's changed attitude to cohabitation no longer warrants the law's refusal to recognise such agreements, particularly if the agreement is one of maintenance within a stable relationship, rather than payment for a sexual relationship (see *post*, p. 136). It is accepted that:

"When an illegitimate child has been born, there is certainly nothing contrary to public policy in the parents coming to an agreement, which they intend to be binding in law, for the maintenance of the child and the mother." (Scarman L.J. in *Horrocks* v. *Forray* (1976).)

Moreover, the law now recognises agreements relating to the home by virtue of the "trust" and "licence" concepts so as to confer rights on a cohabitee whose name does not appear on the title documents, and a duty to support is recognised indirectly by granting a share in the home to a cohabitee who has contributed to its acquisition (see Chapter 2). Similar principles have been applied to property other than the home, for example, savings.

SAVINGS

Where cohabitees have separate incomes and maintain separate accounts, then generally each will be entitled to his or her income and savings. The position is more complicated if they operate a joint savings fund. To what share is each entitled should the cohabitation cease, either by break-up or on death? Most of the reported cases have concerned savings belonging to spouses, but it can be argued that savings belonging to cohabitees should be treated in the same way.

Many couples have joint bank accounts or joint building society accounts. If the account is in joint names and is one into which both parties pay their incomes and from which both take out money, the fund belongs to them jointly and they are known legally as "joint tenants beneficially" (see *ante*, p. 12). Such accounts are sometimes referred to as a "common purse" (see *Jones* v. *Maynard* (1951)). On breakdown of the cohabitation, the fund (or debt if there is an overdraft) belongs to the parties equally and not in the proportions in which they contributed. On death of either of the parties, the "right of survivorship" operates (see Chapter 5) and the survivor is entitled to the balance of the account. By regarding such accounts as belonging to the parties jointly, the law is purporting to give effect to the parties' intentions. It will do so, only in so far as their intentions do not indicate something other than joint ownership. It is advisable, therefore, for the parties to spell out their intentions when the account is opened. This can be done quite simply by a short written statement, of which both parties keep a signed and dated copy, that the account is intended for their joint use and is to be regarded as owned by them jointly.

Property bought with money withdrawn from a joint account will generally belong not to the parties jointly, but to the person who bought it, unless the property was intended for their joint use.

If the parties wish to be regarded as owning separate shares (not necessarily a half each), they should make this clear, in which case they will jointly own the fund as "beneficial tenants in common" and not as beneficial joint tenants (see *ante*, p. 13). On death of either party the right of survivorship does not operate and the deceased's share passes in accordance with his will or the law of intestacy.

Where only one party contributes to an account in joint names, this may be evidence that the parties did not intend a joint interest and that the fund belongs to the person who paid the money in. The principle whereby ownership "results" to the person who provided the money is known as the principle of "resulting trust" (see *ante*, p. 15). Where only one party so contributes, this presumption will operate unless there is evidence to the contrary, so if the parties intend that they should have a joint interest they should make this clear. Thus, if only one of the parties has an income and the income is paid into a joint account so that the other can draw on the account as a matter of convenience, the money in the account belongs to the contributor. An account which was originally opened in joint names for convenience may become a common purse, if the contributor changes his intention so as to benefit the other party (*Re Figgis* (1968)).

The fact that a savings account is in the name of one cohabitee alone does not necessarily mean that the other has no claim to a share. The fund will belong to the party in whose name the account is held, unless there is evidence that it was intended to belong to both jointly. In *Paul* v. *Constance* (1977), a cohabitee successfully claimed half the money in a deposit account opened in the sole name of her partner who had since died. On many occasions he had said that the money was as much hers as his. The court decided that his words showed that he had declared a trust in which both of them had an interest. In effect, he had declared himself trustee of the money in the account for them both in equal shares.

Ownership of savings from a housekeeping fund "result" to the party providing the fund. Cohabitees are not included within special rules which apply to such funds made by a husband, for the expenses of the matrimonial home, or for similar purposes, in which case the money is regarded as belonging to the husband and wife equally, unless they have made alternative arrangements (Married Women's Property Act 1964, s. 1).

WELFARE BENEFITS

The law treats cohabitees as independent persons for maintenance purposes, but it does not follow, therefore, that they are to be treated independently for purposes of welfare benefits. There is a tendency for them to be treated independently if to do so is to their disadvantage, but not if it is to their advantage. There is not the scope within this book to undertake a general consideration of social security law, so the following is an examination of the special rules which apply in cases of cohabitation.

1. *Supplementary Benefit*

Individual claims to supplementary benefit are decided by benefit officers (Supplementary Benefits Act 1976, s. 2, as amended by Social Security Act 1980), who for that purpose have replaced the Supplementary Benefits Commission, which has been abolished (1980 Act, s. 6 (2)). The advisory role of the Commission has been taken over by the Social Security Advisory Committee (1980 Act, s. 9).

The sources of supplementary benefits law are Acts of Parliament and regulations. The supplementary benefits scheme has depended not only on legislation and regulations, but also on discretionary powers conferred by the legislation and regulations. The rules governing the exercise of these discretionary powers have not, in the past, been published, but there is available to the public a useful guide to a claimant's rights, contained in the "Supplementary Benefits Handbook" available from H.M.S.O. The Handbook describes, for the benefit of social workers and others, how the scheme works and how the discretionary powers are applied. It must be stressed that the Handbook is a guide to policy and, as it states: "It is not, however, and must not be treated as a complete and authoritative statement of the law in relation to either classes of cases or any particular case."

Changes in the administration of supplementary benefit, as a result of the Social Security Act 1980, include the publication of the rules and policies applied in determining how much benefit people receive. The rules and policies contain much of what was previously in the Handbook. The changes, which are based on a review of the supplementary benefits scheme published in a report entitled "Social Assistance," mean that entitlement to benefit is generally based on public regulations rather than on discretion. In this respect the change is to be welcomed, for those involved with benefit claims, whether as claimant or social worker, have justifiably had difficulty distinguishing between the law and the discretionary powers conferred by the law.

Who is entitled to benefit?

Everyone in Great Britain over the age of 16, whose resources are insufficient to meet his requirements, is entitled, with certain exceptions and restrictions, to supplementary benefit (Supplementary Benefits Act 1976, s. 1, as amended by Social Security Act 1980). Benefit is called a supplementary pension if paid to a pensioner (and in due course will apply to "one of a married or unmarried couple of whom one is or both are over the age of 65"). In any other case it is called a supplementary allowance.

One of the restrictions imposed by the legislation affects cohabitees and in this respect a couple living together as husband and wife are treated as though they are married. It is provided that:

"Where two persons are a married or unmarried couple, their requirements and resources shall be aggregated and treated—
    (a) until the prescribed date, as those of the man; and
    (b) on and after that date, as those of such one of them as satisfies prescribed conditions or, where both of them satisfy or neither of them satisfies those conditions, as those of such one of them as they may jointly nominate in accordance with regulations or, in default of such a nomination, as the Secretary of State may determine." (1976 Act, Sched. 1, para. 3 (1), as amended by 1980 Act);

and
"Where, ... the requirements and resources of any person fall to be aggregated with, and treated as, those of another person, that other person only shall be entitled to supplementary benefit." (1976 Act, s. 1 (2).)

Currently, therefore, only the man of an unmarried couple can claim benefit for the couple, and only then if he is not in full-time employment (1976 Act, s. 6 (1) as amended). The woman cannot claim benefit for herself. The rule also results in occasional disqualification of men through cohabitation, where the woman's resources exceed their requirements.

After the "prescribed date" (November 1983), cohabitees' resources and requirements will still be aggregated but not necessarily treated as those of the man. This change is in line with an EEC Directive on equal treatment for men and women in social security benefits. The 1980 Act and regulations made thereunder will, in due course, remove some but not all aspects of discrimination against married and cohabiting women.

An "unmarried couple means a man and a woman who are not married to each other but are living together as husband and wife otherwise than in prescribed circumstances" (1976 Act, s. 34, as amended by 1980 Act). The Supplementary Benefit (Aggregation) Regulations 1980 prescribe the circumstances in which persons are not an unmarried couple within the meaning of section 34 (reg. 6), and have replaced the power not to aggregate in "exceptional circumstances." Regulation 6 preserves the practice of an adjustment period where there is a child in the household who is not the child of the man. The adjustment period, during which benefit is paid, is temporary and does not usually extend beyond four weeks, after which benefit is stopped.

A "married couple means a man and a woman who are married to each other and are members of the same household" (s. 34 as amended). The 1980 Regulations prescribe the circumstances in which married couples are to be treated as being, or not being, members of the same household (see reg. 2).

The reasoning behind this so-called "cohabitation rule" is that an unmarried couple should not be more favourably treated than a married couple, which they would if they were able to claim as single persons. In a report published by the Supplementary Benefits Commission entitled "Living Together as Husband and Wife," it was concluded that the rule was still necessary because:

> "... it would be unjustifiable for the State to provide an income for the woman who has the support of a man to whom she is not actually married when it is not provided for the married woman" (para. 100).

The rule, of course, assumes that the man is supporting the woman. The law, however, recognises no support obligation between cohabitees (see *ante*, p. 36). If a husband fails to support his wife, she can enforce her right to maintenance. A cohabitee has no such right. If a couple are cohabiting as man and wife and the man does not support the woman and she is incapable of supporting herself, she is entitled neither to maintenance nor to supplementary benefit. It is not surprising, therefore, that there have been calls to rationalise the system. The number of couples living together as husband and wife is not known, but on the basis of figures given in "Living Together as Husband and Wife," there are about 8,000 cases a year in which benefit is refused or withdrawn because of cohabitation. The cost of abolishing the rule would be considerable.

The cohabitation rule applies to an unmarried couple living together as husband and wife (see above), *i.e.* stable cohabitation relationships. The rule does not apply, therefore, to family cohabitations or to homosexual cohabitations (see Chapter 1). The phrase "living together as husband and wife" has been taken to be synonymous with the earlier phrase "cohabiting as man and wife." The change was proposed because:

"... the term 'cohabitation' has come to acquire a perjorative meaning in the public mind, and its use tends to perpetuate the mistaken assumption that the benefit rule is somehow intended to be a punishment for misconduct" ("Living Together . . .," para. 52).

If a couple admit that there is cohabitation, there is no difficulty. Where it is denied, then in deciding what constitutes "cohabitation," for the purpose of the rule, certain criteria have been laid down.

Members of the same household

For the rule to operate, it is essential that the couple live together in the same household (see, for example, *R. (G.) 11/55*). This does not mean, however, that all couples living in the same household will be cohabiting, for the man could be a lodger, or the woman a housekeeper. The couple must regularly live in the same house or flat, apart from absences in connection with work or visits to relatives, etc., and the man must usually have no other home.

Other factors are dispensable but have been decisive in certain cases in indicating a stable cohabitation, for example:

(i) *Length of the cohabitation.* If the relationship is of a temporary nature, the couple are unlikely to be living together as husband and wife, for that implies more than an occasional or brief relationship. No time limits are laid down and each case depends upon its own facts, but it is expected that a couple will decide within weeks rather than months that they are living together as husband and wife. In some cases it may be apparent from the outset that the relationship is that of husband and wife. A couple's continued living together is strong evidence that the relationship has become that of husband and wife.

(ii) *Financial arrangements.* If one of the parties is financially dependent upon the other, this will go some way to establishing cohabitation, although such evidence is not conclusive. Likewise, the fact that the parties retain financial independence is not conclusive evidence that the relationship is not one of cohabitation. Payment for board and lodging will normally be evidence that the parties are not living as husband and wife.

(iii) *Sexual relationship.* Sexual intercourse is a normal part of marriage and so the fact that a couple have a sexual relationship is, in practice, of great importance in showing that they are living as husband and wife. The relationship as a whole must be considered, so the fact of a sexual relationship does not automatically mean that the couple must be regarded as so living. Failure to establish a sexual relationship will not necessarily rule out such a finding, but if there is no evidence of a sexual relationship, it will be rare for the couple to be considered as living together as husband and wife, unless an analogy can be drawn with a companionship marriage of an elderly couple. Actual proof of a sexual relationship is unnecessary if it can be inferred from the circumstances in which the couple are living together.

(iv) *Children.* The birth of children of the relationship will go a long way towards establishing that the parents are living together as husband and wife, particularly if the man is caring for the children. Likewise, if the man is caring for the woman's children of whom he is not the father.

(v) *Public acknowledgment.* The fact that the couple are known publicly as husband and wife and the woman uses the man's surname, will indicate that they are living as husband and wife (see, for example, *R. (G.) 5/68*). It does not follow, however, that the fact that a couple do not represent themselves as married means they cannot be so regarded (see, for example, *C.P. 97/49*).

It may be that in the light of these factors a decision can be reached as to the nature of the relationship, but inevitably there will be doubtful cases. The National Insurance Commissioners' case law, examples of which are referred to, is helpful for supplementary benefit purposes but not necessarily followed.

If a couple deny that they are living together as husband and wife, it is in practice up to them to prove that they are not, for once it has been decided that they are cohabiting, benefit will be withdrawn, leaving the couple to appeal (see *post*, p. 47). Likewise, once cohabitation has been established, if it later ends, it is up to the claimant to prove that it has ended, which is very difficult if the couple still live together (see, for example, *R. (P.) 6/52*).

In the past the cohabitation rule has been subject to an overriding discretion in cases of urgent need (1976 Act, s. 4), for example, if the claimant's partner fails or refuses to support her, but such payments have not been readily available to cohabitees. The 1980 Act makes new provision for cases of urgent need and regulations may prescribe urgent cases.

Entitlement to benefit is also affected where a person is responsible for another person and they are not a married or unmarried couple, for example, where there is a child under 16 living with the claimant. In such cases the child's requirements and resources must be aggregated with those of the claimant. The requirements and resources of children aged 16 to 19 living with the claimant and receiving full-time education at a recognised establishment, must also be aggregated if, as is usual, they are not entitled to supplementary benefit (1976 Act, Sched. 1, para. 3 (2), as amended by 1980 Act). The 1976 Act and regulations further provide for the circumstances in which a person is to be treated as responsible for another and the prescribed circumstances in which resources and requirements are to be aggregated (see Sched. 1, para. 3 (2) and the Supplementary Benefit (Aggregation) Regulations 1980, regs. 3–5).

In *Supplementary Benefits Commission* v. *Jull, Y.* v. *Supplementary Benefits Commission* (1980), the House of Lords, reversing two High Court decisions, held that on the original wording of the 1976 Act, Sched. 1, para. 3 (2), payments made by the father of an illegitimate child under an affiliation order (see Chapter 6), for the maintenance of a child living with its mother, had to be aggregated with the mother's resources for the purpose of determining the mother's benefit. The change of wording introduced by the 1980 Act was designed to the same effect, in case the two High Court decisions had been affirmed. The result in such cases is that payments made by the father will benefit the State rather than the child.

Claiming benefit

"Parliament clearly intended that the supplementary benefits scheme should be administered in such a way that people would be encouraged to come forward and claim their right to benefit, in the confident expectation that they would be received with courtesy and understanding and that their claims would be decided with scrupulous fairness." ("Living Together . . .," para. 78).

Such is the theory of the scheme. The claim procedure is simple. The initial claim can be made by completing a form available at any post office or local social security office, by letter to the manager of the local social security office or in an urgent case, by calling in person at the local office.

Once a claim has been made, the claimant will either be visited at home by a local social security officer or called for an appointment at the local office, to obtain such information as is necessary for the claim to be assessed, including whether the claimant is living as a member of someone else's household, or is the householder. If a person of the opposite sex is living in the same household, the claimant will be asked whether that person is a "dependant, a boarder, housekeeper or whatever" ("Living Together . . .," paras. 81–82).

It is not official policy for officers to ask questions about sleeping arrangements or a sexual relationship. Official policy, however, does not always filter down properly to local level. Where there is doubt as to whether or not a couple are living together as husband and wife, a specially trained officer will deal with the claim:

> "He explains the position fully to the claimant, who is given a leaflet reinforcing the explanation and encouraged to state fully what his or her position is. Any decision that the claimant is living as a wife (or husband) is taken by a senior officer in the light of the claimant's statement and the trained officer's report. The decision is fully explained to the claimant who is reminded of the right of appeal" (*Handbook*, para. 2.13).

The right of appeal against refusal of benefit is discussed later (see *post*, p. 47).

Withdrawal of benefit

The cohabitation rule has aroused much opposition, particularly in cases where a woman has had an occasional visitor, as a result of which her benefit has been withdrawn. In such cases, where there is no cohabitation, the claimant should appeal (see *post*, p. 47).

Where it is suspected that a couple are cohabiting, a special investigator will be instructed to carry out enquiries. Investigators have no right to enter private premises, except by invitation, but they may well watch the house or make enquiries of the neighbours. Information is often received from informants. The official policy is that investigators are employed only where there is good reason to believe that the claimant may be deliberately concealing or misrepresenting the facts about the relationship.

If benefit is withdrawn, the decision must be given in writing to the claimant, together with a copy of her own statement and details of any information on which the decision is based. The claimant must be notified also of the right of appeal. If false statements have been made, or false documents produced for the purpose of obtaining benefit, the claimant, in addition to having benefit withdrawn, may be prosecuted and, if convicted, be liable for up to three months' imprisonment and/or a fine not exceeding £400 (1976 Act, s. 21 as amended). On the basis of figures given in "Living Together as Husband and Wife," of the 8,000 cases a year in which benefit is refused or withdrawn because of cohabitation (see *ante*, p. 43), 4,000 are after investigation and more than 400 claimants are convicted each year for making false representations about the members of their household.

The effects of withdrawal of benefit can, of course, be serious, even to the extent of the breakdown of cohabitation, in which case the cohabitation bar to benefit will no longer operate and, to that extent, investigation will have proved counter-productive.

Where benefit is withdrawn because of cohabitation and there is any likelihood of children suffering neglect because of the withdrawal, the social security officers should bring the case to the attention of the local authority Social Services Department (see further, "Living Together . . .," paras. 35–48). Regrettably this has not occurred in as many cases as it ought and:

". . . one of the most common reasons given for the failure to refer cases to social workers was the feeling that social workers, more especially at junior level, were hostile to the 'cohabitation rule' and tended to take the view that the Commission was trying to shuffle off its responsibilities on to the Social Services Departments" ("Living Together . . .," para. 37).

Co-operation and close liaison between social security staff and Social Services Departments is essential, not only at national level, where regular meetings are held between the social security authorities and representatives of the Association of Directors of Social Services and with the British Association of Social Workers, but more particularly at local level, for it is here that the presence (or absence) of co-operation, helps (or hinders) those in need. The establishment of local liaison arrangements and exchange of staff between social security offices and area social service teams is, therefore, to be welcomed and encouraged.

Appeals

There is a right of appeal to the Supplementary Benefits Appeal Tribunal (S.B.A.T.) against, *inter alia*, the refusal or withdrawal of supplementary benefit (Supplementary Benefit Act 1976, s. 15, as amended by Social Security Act 1980). An appeal must be made in writing to an office of the Department of Health and Social Security, either by letter or on a form obtainable from the Department. It is helpful in the notice of appeal to set out the reasons for the appeal, as well as the decision being appealed against. An appeal should normally be made within 28 days of the original decision, but the Tribunal chairman has a discretion to extend the period if there has been a good reason for the delay.

The first stage in the appeal process is a review of the decision by the local office, to see if it was correctly made. This review may, and frequently does, result in payment of all or part of the benefit claimed, in which case the appeal lapses. If the claimant (now called the appellant) remains dissatisfied, he must appeal against the decision. Unless an appeal lapses it will proceed. In due course, the appellant will be notified of the date, time and place of the appeal hearing, which will usually take place four to six weeks after lodging the appeal, and he will be sent a copy of the information provided for the Tribunal.

The appeal hearing will be in private. The appellant does not have to attend, but has the right to do so and to be accompanied, or represented, by up to two persons, unless the Tribunal consents to more than two, and to call witnesses, for example, a social worker. The travelling and other expenses (including loss of earnings) of the appellant, his representatives and witnesses are refunded. Legal aid, however, is not available and so legal representation is unusual, but legal advice under the "green form scheme" (see Zander, *Social Workers, their Clients and the Law*, Chap. 2) is available for the preparation of the appeal and the drawing up of written submissions. Many organisations will also help, not only with advice, but also with representation, for example, an appellant's trade union, the Child Poverty Action Group, and details should be sought from the local Citizens' Advice Bureau. The benefit officer also has the right to be represented and to call witnesses.

The hearing will take place before a Tribunal of normally three members, a chairman (not usually a lawyer), a member appointed· from a panel nominated by the local County Association of Trades Councils and the other member from a panel appointed by the Secretary of State. The Tribunal may act without one of the members, but not without the chairman and only if the appellant and the benefit officer do not object. A clerk to the Tribunal is also present. There is no set procedure. Often the officer presenting the supplementary benefit case ("the presenting officer") speaks first. The official policy is that he should not see himself as the appellant's adversary, although he may in fact appear so. The appellant, or his representative, speaks after the presenting officer. The parties can question each other and the witnesses, and they may be asked questions by the Tribunal. After all parties have been heard, they will be asked to withdraw so that the Tribunal can consider its decision, notification of which will be sent by post to the parties shortly after the hearing, along with a copy of the record of the proceedings.

There is a right of appeal against a Tribunal decision to a Social Security Commissioner, but only on a point of law (1976 Act, s. 15A, as inserted by Social Security Act 1979, s. 6).

2. *Family Income Supplement*

Family Income Supplement (F.I.S.) was introduced in 1971 by the Family Income Supplement Act 1970, and is normally paid to those in full-time work with at least one dependent child. It is intended for families that are not entitled to supplementary benefit and have a low income.

For F.I.S. purposes a family, as originally defined, is a man or single woman engaged, and normally engaged, in remunerative full-time work; and with at least one dependent child. Where the man's household "includes a woman to whom he is married or who lives with him as his wife," she is included within the family (1970 Act, s. 1 (1)). Cohabitees are treated like spouses. A woman living with a man as his wife is not eligible in her own right. The man must be in full-time work; if she works, but he does not, F.I.S. cannot be claimed. She could claim F.I.S., however, if she were a single woman, *i.e.* not living with a man as his wife, with a dependent child.

The Social Security Act 1980 has redefined a "family" as the following members of a household:

"(a) a man or woman engaged and normally engaged in remunerative full-time work; and

(b) if the person mentioned in the preceding paragraph is one of a married or unmarried couple, the other member of the couple; and

(c) the child or children whose requirements are provided for, in whole or in part, by the person or either of the persons mentioned in the preceding paragraphs

except that persons who include a married or unmarried couple shall not be a family for the purposes of this Act if one of the couple is engaged and normally engaged as aforesaid and the other member of the couple is receiving such payments as may be specified by regulations" (1970 Act, s. 1 (1), as amended by 1980 Act, s. 7).

The change of wording, which is not yet in force, continues to treat an unmarried couple the same as a married couple, but removes the requirement for a woman claimant to be single and provides for equal treatment of the sexes.

An "unmarried couple" is defined as meaning "a man and a woman who are not married to each other but are living together as husband and wife" and a "married couple means a man and a woman who are married to each other and are members of the same household" (1970 Act, s. 17 (1), as amended by 1980 Act, s. 7 (6)). The test of whether or not a couple are living together as husband and wife is the same as that for supplementary benefit (see *ante*, p. 43).

"Full-time work" means more than 30 hours a week; those in temporary or casual work are therefore excluded. A lone parent, or someone bringing up a child or children on their own, may claim if he, or she, works more than 24 hours a week.

The supplement is payable to families with at least one dependent child, who need not be the child of the parties. "Child" for this purpose means a person under 16, or under 19 and receiving full-time education which is not advanced education.

A leaflet (F.I.S. 1), incorporating a claim form, giving details of the scheme and how to claim, is available from social security offices, post offices, Citizens' Advice Bureaux, Social Services Departments and Unemployment Benefit Offices.

The claim must generally be made jointly by the man and woman (1970 Act, s. 5 (2)). F.I.S. is payable if the parties' income is less than the prescribed amount (s. 1 (2)) or "qualifying level" as it is called (see F.I.S. 1). The supplement is half the difference between a family's gross income and the qualifying level, subject to a maximum payment. It is payable normally for 52 weeks, regardless of any change in the family's circumstances. As families which receive supplement have the right to other benefits, it is worth claiming, even if the amount payable is small.

There is a right of appeal to an Appeal Tribunal against any decision of a supplement officer (1970 Act, s. 7 (1), as amended by 1980 Act, s. 7 (4)). The appeal procedure is identical to that for Supplementary Benefits Appeal Tribunals (see *ante*, p. 47). Very few appeals are successful.

3. *Child Benefit*

Child benefit, unlike supplementary benefit and F.I.S., is not a means tested benefit. Entitlement to it, like entitlement to F.I.S., is based on neither marriage nor cohabitation, but on a family including at least one child. Payment is made to a person who is responsible for a child. If more than one person is responsible, for example, cohabitees living together and having a child living with them, only one of them is entitled. The Child Benefit Act 1975 sets out a scheme of priorities (see *post*, p. 121).

4. *Contributory Benefits*

None of the benefits discussed so far depend upon payment of contributions to the National Insurance Scheme (formerly in the form of stamps and currently through P.A.Y.E.). A number of other benefits do depend, however, on such contributions, for example, unemployment benefit, sickness benefit and invalidity benefit. For these benefits, cohabitees are treated as single persons and entitlement is based on the claimant's national insurance contributions.

Cohabitees acquire no national insurance rights as a result of their partner's contributions to the Scheme. This affects entitlement to a number of contributory benefits, for example, maternity grant, death grant and widow's benefit. To qualify for maternity grant, a woman may currently rely on her own contributions or those of her husband (Social Security Act 1975, s. 21 and Sched. 3, para. 2, to be amended, see Social Security Act 1980, s. 5, which provides for maternity grant to become a non-contributory benefit). In the case of cohabitees, if the woman has not paid the requisite contributions, she is not entitled to a grant on the basis of the man's contributions. This current discrimination against unmarried couples does not apply to maternity allowance, which is to compensate the woman for loss of earning power and is payable only on her contributions (1975 Act, s. 22 and Sched. 3, para. 3). Death grant is payable, *inter alia*, in respect of the death of a spouse of a contributor, but not on the death of a cohabitee of a contributor (see *post*, p. 97). Likewise, widow's benefit is payable to a surviving wife, but a cohabitee is entitled to nothing, however long and stable the cohabitation. Moreover, a widow who later cohabits will have her right to benefit suspended during cohabitation (see *post*, p. 96). This long-established cohabitation rule derives from the Widows', Orphans' and Old Age Contributory Pensions Act 1925, s. 21 (1).

Entitlement to a retirement pension depends upon the type of pension. A "Category A" pension is based solely on the claimant's contributions (1975 Act, s. 28). A "Category B" pension is payable to a woman by virtue of her husband's contributions, provided that certain conditions are satisfied (1975 Act, s. 29). No such pension is available by virtue of a cohabitee's contributions.

A child's special allowance, which is only payable to a divorced woman on the basis of her former husband's contributions, and who satisfies the conditions of the 1975 Act, is suspended if she lives with a man, to whom she is not married, as his wife (1975 Act, s. 31, as amended by Social Security (Miscellaneous Provisions) Act 1977, s. 22 (2)).

5. *Non-contributory Benefits*

Some benefits are non-contributory, *i.e.* they are not based on contributions from either the claimant or anyone else, to the National Insurance Scheme. Cohabitation may nevertheless operate to deprive a person of such benefit. Thus, a non-contributory invalidity pension, which is payable to persons incapable of work, is not payable to a married woman residing with her husband or maintained by him, or to an unmarried woman if she and a man are living together as husband and wife, except, in either case, if the woman is incapable of performing normal household duties (1975 Act, s. 36, as amended by 1977 Act, s. 22 (2); Social Security (Non-contributory Invalidity Pensions) Regulations 1977). No distinction is therefore made between married and unmarried couples.

An invalid care allowance, which is to compensate a person for loss of earnings as a result of caring for a severely disabled person, is payable neither to a married woman residing with her husband or maintained by him, nor to an unmarried woman living with a man as his wife (1975 Act, s. 37, as amended by 1977 Act, s. 22 (2)). The exclusion of these married women and female cohabitees is on the questionable basis that they would probably have remained at home anyway. A female party to a family cohabitation, for example a sister looking after an invalid brother, would not be excluded.

These examples offer further illustration of the "heads you win, tails I lose" situation in which cohabitees find themselves regarding welfare benefits, namely that cohabitation is not taken into account when assessing entitlement to benefit (for example, unemployment benefit, maternity grant, death grant, widow's benefit, retirement pension), yet cohabitation may be taken into account to deprive a cohabitee of benefit to which she would have been entitled except for cohabitation (for example, widow's benefit, child's special allowance, non-contributory invalidity pension, invalid care allowance).

There is provision for the increase of certain contributory and non-contributory benefits to compensate a person for maintaining a dependant (see 1975 Act, Chapter III, as amended by Social Security Act 1980). The class of dependants is limited to children and certain adult dependants, *i.e.* spouses, certain relatives and a person who is neither the spouse of the beneficiary (or pensioner) nor a child, and who has the care of a child or children of the beneficiary's (or pensioner's) family (1975 Act, ss. 44 (3) (*c*) and 46 (2), as amended by 1980 Act, Sched. 1, para. 4). The latter category has been referred to as "housekeepers" (see Calvert, *Social Security Law*, pp. 33–34), and was widened by the Social Security Act 1980 from the original category (currently still in force), which was limited to a "female person (not a child)." There is a similar provision for benefit for industrial injuries (1975 Act, s. 66 (1) (*d*), as amended by 1980 Act). The number of cohabitees who will satisfy the conditions of entitlement is limited.

6. *Rent Rebates and Allowances and Rate Rebates*

The operation of these rebates and allowances is discussed in companion works to this book (see Zander, *op. cit.*, Chap. 4 and Arden, *Housing: Security and Rent Control*, pp. 136–139). So far as cohabitation is concerned, the important point to note is that for rent rebates and allowances, the Housing Finance Act 1972 equates cohabitees with a "married couple," for the latter "includes a man and a woman who lives with him as his wife" (Sched. 3, para. 2). Where the parties, whether married or unmarried, live apart they cease to be regarded as a married couple.

If a couple qualify for rent rebates or allowances, they will normally qualify also for rate rebates, because the schemes are linked (see Local Government Act 1974, ss. 11–14).

TAX

The tax system provides a further example of the State's encouragement of marriage and discouragement of cohabitation. The tax reliefs available to a married couple are not available to an unmarried couple living together as husband and wife. For tax purposes, it is generally cheaper, therefore, to be married than to cohabit, for example:

1. *Income Tax*

Cohabitees are treated as single persons for income tax purposes, so the man is not entitled to married man's allowance and both parties remain entitled to the single person's allowance. A married couple, but not an unmarried couple, who are living together and who have not opted for the woman's earned income to be taxed as if she were unmarried, are treated as one unit for income tax (Income and Corporation Taxes Act 1970, s. 37). Their incomes are added together and tax is charged on their joint income as though it was the income of one person. They receive the benefit of the higher personal allowance plus a wife's earned income relief (1970 Act, s. 8). It is only where their joint income is high, or the wife has a high unearned income, that they will be at a disadvantage in being taxed as a married couple, in which case they can jointly elect for separate taxation on their earned income (Finance Act 1971, s. 23). The wife's unearned income is added to the husband's income for tax purposes. Election for separate taxation reduces the disadvantage in being married, but marriage confers no tax benefit. Most couples, however, receive tax benefit by marrying. Moreover, either of a married couple, but not a cohabiting couple, can opt for separate assessment (not the same as separate taxation), whilst retaining the benefit of the higher overall allowance. The tax payable remains the same, but is apportioned between them and each is responsible for the payment of his or her share (1970 Act, ss. 38 and 39).

Cohabitees may be able to benefit from an additional personal allowance if they have a child living with them (Income and Corporation Taxes Act 1970, s. 14 as amended). A person who is not entitled to the higher married person's relief is entitled to this additional allowance if he has a "qualifying child" living with him (see 1970 Act, s. 14 (5)–(8), as inserted by Finance (No. 2) Act 1979, Sched. 1, para. 2). Only one allowance is given irrespective of the number of qualifying children living with him. This relief is particularly beneficial to cohabitees with children and compensates for the lack of the married person's relief. If both cohabitees are entitled to claim, the allowance is divided between them (1970 Act, s. 14A, as inserted by 1979 Act, Sched. 1, para. 3).

2. *Capital Transfer Tax*

Capital transfer tax replaced estate duty and is payable on the value transferred as a result of which the transferor's estate is diminished. It is chargeable on transfers between cohabitees as if they were strangers. They do not receive the benefit of the exemption from tax in respect of transfers between spouses (Finance Act 1975, s. 29 and Sched. 6, para. 1 as amended). Such tax is not chargeable, however, until a person has transferred £50,000 during his life or on death (1975 Act, s. 37 as amended) and there is an additional annual exemption of £2,000 (1975 Act, Sched. 6, para. 2 as amended), so capital transfer tax is unlikely to be a problem to many cohabitees.

3. *Capital Gains Tax*

Capital gains tax is levied on "chargeable gains" on the "disposal of assets" after deducting "allowable losses" (Capital Gains Tax Act 1979, ss. 1, 4 and 19). Special rules apply to disposals between a married couple who are living together, so that neither a gain nor loss accrues to the one making the disposal (1979 Act, s. 44) and thus no tax is payable. The tax is chargeable on the disposal of assets between cohabitees.

A cohabitee does not benefit from the provision that the allowable losses of a wife living with her husband can be applied against the husband's chargeable gains (1979 Act, s. 4 (2)).

In many cohabitations, there will again be no problem, because capital gains tax is only levied on gains in excess of £3,000 in any one year (1979 Act, s. 5 as amended by Finance Act 1980, s. 77), and is unlikely to apply to a disposal of an interest in a house which is owner-occupied (1979 Act, s. 101 as amended).

Further Reading

Bromley, *Family Law* (Butterworths, 5th ed.).

Cretney, *Principles of Family Law* (Sweet and Maxwell, 3rd ed.).

Eekelaar, *Family Law and Social Policy* (Weidenfeld and Nicolson).

Sweet and Maxwell's Family Law Statutes (2nd ed.).

Arden, *Housing: Security and Rent Control* (Sweet and Maxwell).

Bell, *Research Study on Supplementary Benefit Appeal Tribunals* (H.M.S.O. 1975).

Calvert, *Social Security Law* (Sweet and Maxwell, 2nd ed.).

Cohabitation—Report by the Supplementary Benefits Commission to the Secretary of State for Social Services (H.M.S.O. 1971).

EEC Directive on Equal Treatment in Social Security Benefits (Dir. 79/7).

Legal Action Group, *A Guide to Supplementary Benefit Law* (2nd ed.).

Lister, "As Man and Wife? A Study of the Cohabitation Rule" (C.P.A.G. Poverty Research Series No. 2).

Lister, "Social Assistance: A Civil Servant's Review" (1979) J.S.W.L. 133.

"Living Together as Husband and Wife" (Supplementary Benefits Administration Papers 5, H.M.S.O.).

Moon, "The Rights of Cohabitees—3. Money" (1979) Legal Action Group Bulletin 39.

Oliver, "Rationalising the Cohabitation Rule" (1979) 9 Fam. Law 10.

Ogus and Barendt, *Law of Social Security* (Butterworths).

Pearl, "Cohabitation in English Social Security and Supplementary Benefits Legislation" (1979) 9 Fam. Law 232.

Pollard, *Social Welfare Law* (Oyez).

Report of the Committee on Abuse of Social Security Benefits, Cmnd. 5228.

Report of the Committee on One-Parent Families, Cmnd. 5629.

Social Assistance: A Review of the Supplementary Benefits Scheme in Great Britain (DHSS).

Supplementary Benefits Commission Annual Report 1978, Cmnd. 7725.

Supplementary Benefits Handbook (Supplementary Benefits Administration Papers 2).

The Taxation of Husband and Wife (H.M.S.O., 1980).

Zander, *Social Workers, their Clients and the Law* (Sweet and Maxwell, 3rd ed.).

4 Violence

It is recognised that domestic violence is not limited to married partners and that:

> "... a battered wife is a woman who has suffered serious or repeated physical injury from the man with whom she lives." (*Per* Royal College of Psychiatrists, see Report from the House of Commons Select Committee on Violence in Marriage 1975 (hereafter S.C.R.), para. 6.)

The findings of that Committee, along with those in the Finer Report on One-Parent Families, did much to highlight the problems of battered women. The law cannot prevent men from battering women, but it can help the battered woman who is in need of protection. In that respect the law has been totally inadequate, no doubt because:

> "Some people, including some in high places, still scorn the thought of a battered wife. Is it not a husband's right to beat her? Is it not her fault? Should she not just leave? Might she even enjoy being beaten? Such people should not forget that a large percentage of all known murders take place within the family setting: home is for many a very violent place. At least some of those murdered were maltreated wives who did not or could not leave in time." (S.C.R., para. 8).

Until the Domestic Violence and Matrimonial Proceedings Act 1976 (hereafter the 1976 Act) the battered cohabitee was at an even greater disadvantage than the battered wife. Her chief remedy under civil law was to claim damages for assault or trespass and seek an injunction as an ancillary remedy (see *post*, p. 72). Her real need, however, was for immediate protection, not only for herself but for her children. Hence the need for safe accommodation. Yet the courts had no power to order a man out of a house of which he was the owner or tenant, an Englishman's home being his castle. That has now changed.

DOMESTIC VIOLENCE AND MATRIMONIAL PROCEEDINGS ACT 1976

1. *The Law*

The 1976 Act makes an injunction a remedy by itself and thus easier to obtain. It is no longer necessary for a cohabitee to claim damages for assault or trespass. Under the previous law, once the injunction was obtained it was common for the claim for damages to be adjourned indefinitely (see *post*, p. 72).

Orders and applicants

An injunction under the Act directs the other party not to molest the applicant, or a child living with the applicant (non-molestation injunction), or excludes him from the matrimonial home (exclusion injunction) or requires him to let the applicant live in the home (s. 1 (1)). The Act applies equally to a man or a woman. The examples given will have the woman as the applicant, for in the majority of cases the man is the violent partner, although cases of husband battering are not unknown. (On violence generally see Freeman "Violence in the Home," and on battered husbands in particular see Chapter 9.)

The appropriate court is any county court (see *post*, p. 69). It can make any one or more of the orders in s. 1 (1) and it is expressly provided that the section "shall apply to a man and a woman who are living with each other in the same household as husband and wife as it applies to the parties to a marriage and any reference to the matrimonial home shall be construed accordingly" (s. 1 (2)). The Act refers to parties "who are living with each other." Does it apply, therefore, to the battered woman who has been driven out of the home and then seeks the protection of the Act? The courts have not taken the literal interpretation and have applied the Act provided that the cohabitation existed until the events which led to the application being made. (See, for example, *B* v. *B* (1978), *Davis* v. *Johnson* (1978), *McLean* v. *Nugent* (1979).) This interpretation seems correct, otherwise much of the good of the Act would have been undone. Except in these circumstances, however, the Act will not apply once there has been a break in the relationship, in which event the applicant will have to rely on the pre-Act remedies (see *post*, p. 72).

Not only must the parties be living with each other but they must also be doing so "in the same household as husband and wife." By using the analogy with the husband and wife relationship, the Act limits its application to those who are cohabiting on a stable basis. The Act has been inaccurately described as protecting battered mistresses. The need for a stable relationship was stressed by Lord Kilbrandon in the House of Lords in *Davis* v. *Johnson*:

> "It is unfortunate that the Act has been described, in popular language, as an attempt to protect 'battered mistresses.' The English language is poor in this context. 'Mistress,' having lost its respectable if not reverential significance, came to mean a woman

installed, in a clandestine way, by someone of substance, normally married, for his intermittent sexual enjoyment. This class of woman, if indeed she still exists, is not dealt with by the 1976 Act at all. The subsection was included for the protection of families (households in which a man and a woman either do or do not bring up children), the man and the woman being, for whatever reason, unmarried. . . . I do not know a single English word which will accurately describe the unmarried housewife, but that is what Parliament is talking about."

Likewise, family cohabitations, for example a brother and sister living together, are not included. Parties to a void marriage will be protected (for the grounds on which a marriage is void see Matrimonial Causes Act 1973, s. 11) except if the marriage is void because the parties are not male and female (M.C.A. 1973, s. 11 (*c*), as occurred in *Corbett* v. *Corbett* (1970)). The reference in the Act to a "man and a woman" excludes any application by a party to a homosexual cohabitation.

The fact that the parties are living under the same roof does not necessarily mean that they satisfy the requirement of living "in the same household as husband and wife." The smaller the home, however, the more difficult it is for the parties to live in separate households. In *Adeoso* v. *Adeoso* (1981) an unmarried couple lived as man and wife in a flat consisting of one bedroom, a sitting-room, a kitchen and a bathroom. Their relationship broke up. Mr. Adeoso slept in the sitting-room and Mrs. Adeoso slept in the bedroom. They kept their rooms locked. She stopped cooking for him or washing his clothes. They did not speak to one another and communicated by written notes. They continued to share the rent and the cost of the electricity. Mrs. Adeoso applied to the court under the 1976 Act because of Mr. Adeoso's alleged violence. The county court judge decided he could not hear her application because the parties were not living together as husband and wife and hence the Act did not apply. The Court of Appeal allowed Mrs. Adeoso's appeal against the judge's finding. The fact that they lived behind locked doors in separate rooms in a flat with only two rooms did not amount to living separately. Had the home been large enough to be divided into separate parts it would be different.

It is only possible to seek an injunction against "the other party." If one partner should bring a new partner into the home, the former partner has no remedy under the Act against the newcomer. Similarly the Act cannot be used against friends or relatives of the other party. If a spouse, therefore, takes a mistress or lover and they cohabit in the matrimonial home, the 1976 Act gives no remedy to the other spouse against the mistress or lover. The Act is, however, "without prejudice to the jurisdiction of the High Court" (s. 1 (1)), to which an aggrieved spouse would have to apply and there are pre-Act examples of a wife being granted an injunction by the High Court ordering her husband's mistress out of the matrimonial home. In *Adams* v. *Adams* (1965) the wife was granted such an injunction to protect the interests of the children but not her own interests. There have been cases where the court was prepared to order the mistress out in order to protect the wife's interest (*Pinckney* v. *Pinckney* (1966), *Jones* v. *Jones* (1971)). Such orders are not available, however, under the 1976 Act.

Molestation

The Act's title refers to "Domestic Violence" but its object is to give protection against molestation. To obtain a non-molestation injunction (but not necessarily an exclusion injunction) the applicant must prove molestation. What constitutes molestation? In a pre-Act case (*Vaughan* v. *Vaughan* (1973)), a husband pestered his wife. He would call on her early in the morning and late at night, both at home and work, making a nuisance of himself the whole time. There was no violence but he knew that she was frightened of him. There was medical evidence that the husband's pestering had affected his wife's health. He argued that his conduct did not amount to molestation. The Court of Appeal held that it did. Violence is not therefore necessary, although the applicant's case will be that much stronger if there is evidence of violence. Molestation will include "mental cruelty" as it used to be called, *i.e.* injury to mental health and, it is submitted, the courts should be prepared to extend molestation to cases where there is a reasonable apprehension of injury to health. The presence or absence of violence is, however, important under section 2 of the 1976 Act when it comes to the question of breach of an injunction. Section 2 (see *post*, p. 66) is expressly qualified by a reference to violence. Section 1 is not so qualified. Moreover it is only where a "non-molestation injunction" is sought (*i.e.* under s. 1 (1) (*a*) or (*b*)) that molestation need be proved, for in *Spindlow* v. *Spindlow* (1979) (see *post*, p. 65) the Court of Appeal made the point that the provisions in section 1 relating to exclusion from the home do not refer to molestation. As the unmarried Mr. Spindlow had not molested the unmarried Mrs. Spindlow the court could not make a non-molestation injunction. The court did, however, grant an "exclusion injunction," excluding Mr. Spindlow from the home. The decision seems surprising, for it means that neither violence nor molestation need be proved for an exclusion injunction. Consideration is given later as to what is needed (see *post*, p. 64). Protection against molestation is also given to any child who is living with the applicant. The courts are always anxious to protect the interests of children. The only restriction in section 1 is that the child must be living with the applicant. A child living with the other party is unprotected. There is no requirement that the child be a child of the applicant or of the other party, so, for example, a foster child will be protected. The definition is thus wider than that of "child of the family" in matrimonial legislation. There could be difficulties when interpreting "living with the applicant" as the Act does not define "living with." With whom is a child living when he is at boarding school or in hospital? Is the phrase to be given the same meaning as references in the Children Act 1975 to "the person with whom a child has his home," *i.e.* "actual custody"? In which case absence of the child at hospital or boarding school or any other temporary absence is to be disregarded (Children Act 1975, s. 87).

Exclusion

The most significant provisions are those enabling a court to exclude a cohabitee from the home (s. 1 (1) (*c*)) or requiring one cohabitee to allow the other to enter and remain in the home (s. 1 (1) (*d*)). In either case the order may relate to all or part of the home and an order under section 1 (1) (*c*) can apply not only to the home but also to a specified locality in which the home is situate. A section 1 (1) (*d*) order will often be made in conjunction with a section 1 (1) (*c*) order.

Any reference in subsection 1 to the matrimonial home includes a house in which a man and a woman are living with each other as husband and wife (s. 1 (2)). The Act only applies therefore to a household in which the parties are living (or in certain circumstances have lived, see *ante*, p. 58) as husband and wife. So if one party to a cohabitation leaves the common home and sets up home elsewhere the new home is not covered. Likewise, if a spouse leaves the matrimonial home and cohabits with someone else in a new home, the other spouse will have no action over the new home as it cannot constitute the matrimonial home. If the leaving spouse wishes to protect the interests of himself and his cohabitee in the new home against the other spouse, he also cannot use the 1976 Act and will have to have recourse to the High Court (for the situation envisaged see *Nanda* v. *Nanda* (1967)).

The court's powers under the 1976 Act to make orders in respect of the home are irrespective of property rights. This has been settled by the House of Lords (*Davis* v. *Johnson*). The Act's effectiveness was initially weakened considerably by two decisions of the Court of Appeal (*B* v. *B* (1978) and *Cantliff* v. *Jenkins* (1978)). It was held that the Act was procedural only and did not alter the substantive law affecting parties' rights to occupy premises. The court could not order out a party who had a proprietary interest, whether as sole owner, joint owner, sole tenant (as in *B* v. *B*) or joint tenant (as in *Cantliff* v. *Jenkins*).

The Court of Appeal said that only if the applicant was the sole owner or sole tenant could the other party be excluded. The ruling, which made an empty shell of the Act, was shortlived. In *Davis* v. *Johnson* a specially constituted Court of Appeal refused to follow its earlier decisions. By a majority of three to two it held that an injunction excluding the other party (the respondent) from the home could be granted irrespective of property rights. The case is an important one. It involved a couple who were joint tenants of a council flat. They were cohabitees and the applicant was the mother of the respondent's child. She was subjected to extreme violence by him and was so frightened that she fled with the child to the battered wives' refuge at Chiswick. She applied for an order under the 1976 Act that she be allowed to return to the flat and the respondent be excluded from it. A county court judge granted her application, then *B* v. *B* and *Cantliff* v. *Jenkins* were decided and, because of these decisions, another county court judge rescinded the injunction excluding the respondent from the home. The applicant then appealed to the Court of Appeal which restored the original order. The law was in a state of confusion and not surprisingly the respondent appealed to the House of Lords. His appeal was dismissed, and the decision of the Court of Appeal affirmed. So, a battered cohabitee with no property rights in the home can apply for an injunction to exclude his or her partner, even if the party against whom the order is sought is the sole owner or sole tenant of the home. A cohabitee now has similar rights to those of a spouse to expel a violent partner, albeit that the former's right solely arises out of the 1976 Act, whereas the latter enjoys that right by reason of the marriage, as well as the rights conferred by the 1976 Act. This seems correct. The spouse's additional rights arise out of the marriage relationship, a relationship which the cohabitee has not entered into. So a wife has the benefit of the Matrimonial Homes Act 1967 and, if there are matrimonial proceedings, the matrimonial causes legislation (see *post*, p. 130). Moreover, the remaining two substantive sections of the 1976 Act (ss. 3 and 4) do not apply to unmarried couples. Sections 1 and 2 of the 1976 Act are the nub of the Act, however, and their strength is in the protection conferred on the unmarried, for the Act has not significantly changed the nature of spouses' rights, but it has provided a better procedure for their enforcement. Further consideration will be given to the nature of the rights given to cohabitees shortly (see *post*, p. 63).

The notion that an Englishman's home is his castle and within it he may do what he likes to whomsoever he likes has been eroded one step further, whether the Englishman be married or not. In the words of Sir George Baker, former President of the Family Division, in response to a circuit judge's protest at the extension of protection to cohabitees:

"... I cannot see why, as a doctor does not pause to ask if the lady is married before tending her broken nose, the judge should ask the question before trying to stop a repetition."

An exclusion injunction granted under the 1976 Act does not affect the legal rights of ownership to the home but only the enjoyment of those rights. It gives a right of occupation. Referring to section 1, Lord Scarman in *Davis* v. *Johnson* said:

> "The purpose of the section is not to create rights but to strengthen remedies. Subsection (2) does, however, confer on the unmarried woman with no property in the home a new right. Though enjoying no property right to possession of the family home, she can apply to the county court for an order restricting or suspending for a time her family partner's right to possession of the premises and conferring on her a limited right of occupancy."

The purpose of the order has been seen as a form of temporary and not permanent relief, although there have been cases where the order was of a permanent nature (see *Spindlow* v. *Spindlow*, *post*, p. 65). This temporary relief is to enable the applicant to find other accommodation. How long, therefore, does such an injunction last? The period is at the discretion of the court, but a *Practice Note* of July 21, 1978 states that consideration should be given to imposing a time limit, and that in most cases a period of up to three months will be sufficient, at least to start with. The respondent can, of course, apply within the period for a discharge of the injunction, for example if the parties are reconciled. Likewise the applicant can apply for an extension. An injunction under section 1 of the 1976 Act is therefore to be regarded as essentially a short-term remedy (see also *Hopper* v. *Hopper* (1979)).

As the applicant acquires no property rights but only a limited personal right, there is nothing to prevent the respondent, if he is sole owner or sole tenant, from selling, letting or assigning the property, unless the applicant has any independent property rights (see Chapter 2), but to do so would take some time and as Lord Salmon said in the House of Lords, it:

> "... would accordingly prevent the former mistress [*sic*] from being thrown out without giving her any breathing space in which to look for suitable accommodation. And this, I believe, is the major object which the Act sought to achieve, first aid but not intensive care for 'battered wives.'"

So the right of occupation given to the unmarried woman is not as extensive as that already enjoyed by a wife under the Matrimonial Homes Act 1967. Under that Act a wife can register her right of occupation which is then protected even against third parties (see *ante*, p. 26).

The owner or tenant cohabitee wishing to dispose of the home would, of course, be faced with the practical difficulty of being unable to give vacant possession and whilst the injunction is in operation he would be unable to obtain an order for possession of the premises. If the owner or tenant did sell, let or assign to a third party despite the existence of the injunction, the third party could presumably obtain an order for possession, as the injunction does not bind third parties.

There is also the problem of the contents of the home. Orders relate to the home, not its contents. So, for example, when Miss Davis returned to the home which Mr. Johnson had been ordered to vacate, she was greeted by bare floorboards. Whilst it can be argued that the duty on a husband to house his wife extends to the provision of basic household necessities (see Freeman, *op. cit.*, p. 204) there is no duty to house a cohabitee.

What is the position of a tenant ordered out of his rented property? If the tenancy is a private one rather than a council tenancy can the injunction have the effect of terminating the tenancy? The 1976 Act is silent on the question. The answer ought to be no, otherwise the protected party would be in danger of losing that protection. It has been suggested (Martin, "Domestic Violence and the Rent Acts" (1978)) that the survival of the tenancy must depend on the general case law (see *ante*, Chapter 2) in which case the decision in *Lloyd* v. *Sadler* (1978) supports the view that the tenancy would continue. If the tenancy does continue then the excluded tenant will remain liable for his obligations to the landlord, for example to pay the rent, and, arguably to the public authorities, for example the rating authority, the gas, electricity and water boards.

Where the tenancy is a council tenancy the decision in *Spindlow* v. *Spindlow* (*post,* p. 65) suggests a preparedness for the court to take on the role of housing authority, for in the words of Ormrod L.J. in that case:

> "Parliament has ... put on to the court the responsibility for making the decision, which was previously left with the housing authority. Now that the court has jurisdiction it may be more convenient and better that the court should adjudicate rather than that some administrative adjudication should be made."

A distinction was drawn between a house owned by one of the cohabitees or subject to a private tenancy, in which case the appropriate order may be a temporary one, and a council house, in which case the same considerations do not apply.

Considerations when granting an injunction

An important question for any applicant is what factors will the court take into account when deciding whether or not to grant a non-molestation injunction or an exclusion injunction? In *Spindlow* v. *Spindlow* (1979) the Court of Appeal said that as, for the purposes of the 1976 Act, unmarried couples are to be treated in the same way as married couples, the court's discretion under section 1 to exclude a party from the house is to be exercised according to the same principles as the High Court exercises the jurisdiction to eject a spouse from the home. The case involved an unmarried couple who were joint tenants of a council house. They had an 18-month-old child and the woman (the applicant) had a three-year-old child by a former marriage. The applicant and the children left the family home and she applied for an order excluding the respondent from the house. The judge found that there had been no serious violence or adverse conduct by the respondent but that the parties' relationship had definitely come to an end. He decided that the fair and practicable solution, in the interests of the children, was to exclude the respondent from the house. He granted an exclusion injunction and an injunction restraining the respondent from molesting the applicant or the children. The respondent appealed. The Court of Appeal discharged the non-molestation injunction because there was no evidence that Mr. Spindlow had molested Mrs. Spindlow (see *ante*, p. 60). Evidence of molestation was, however, said to be unnecessary for an exclusion injunction and so that part of the appeal relating to Mr. Spindlow's exclusion was dismissed. The conclusion, therefore, is that an applicant must show more for a non-molestation injunction than for an exclusion injunction. If correct, this is surprising, for traditionally the courts have been reluctant to make exclusion orders, preferring instead the less drastic and, it is suggested, less effective, non-molestation injunction (see, for example, *Montgomery* v. *Montgomery* (1964)).

In considering whether or not to make the exclusion injunction in *Spindlow* the court applied section 1 as though it were being applied to a married couple. Reference was thus made to the important case of *Bassett* v. *Bassett* (1975) where the Court of Appeal said that the court should think in terms of homes, especially for the children, and then balance the hardship between the spouses. The balance will usually tip in favour of the party looking after the children. So, in *Spindlow* the welfare of the children and the provision of a home for them was stressed as the court's primary concern. Had there been no children the parties could, in the words of the court, "be left to get on with it." There were two small children in need of a home and the only person whom the court considered could provide it was Mrs. Spindlow. Thus the unfortunate Mr. Spindlow had to leave. The case was seen as a housing matter, particularly housing for the children. (See also *Rennick* v. *Rennick* (1978), *Spearing* v. *Spearing* (1978).)

In ordering Mr. Spindlow to leave, the court was doing more than making a temporary order of the type suggested in *Davis* v. *Johnson*. It was effectively reallocating the tenancy and thus making the decision which was previously left with the housing authority. A crucial factor, therefore, is the type of property (see *ante*, p. 64). If, as in *Spindlow*, the parties are council tenants the court seems more willing to make a permanent order. If, however, the tenancy is a private one, or the property is owned by one of the parties then the court will be inclined to make temporary adjustments pending alternative arrangements being made. There is a danger in the *Spindlow* type of case, a danger recognised by the court, that "a malicious girl with a child or children could oust her man friend from the house by merely walking out and putting up a bogus case."

Prior to the decision in *Bassett* the case law on husband and wife injunctions suggested a reluctance on the part of the courts to make such orders. So, in *Hall* v. *Hall* (1971) an exclusion order was described as a most drastic one, which ought not to be made unless it proved impossible for the parties to live together. Unpleasantness or inconvenience were thought not to be sufficient grounds for ordering a spouse out of the house. It is suggested that the better approach is that in *Bassett*, *i.e.* it should be "strictly practical having regard to the realities of family life" and the court should think essentially in terms of homes for the children. Indeed it has been suggested that the use of the words "impossible" and "intolerable" in the context of applications for orders excluding a party from the matrimonial home should stop (*Walker* v. *Walker* (1978)).

Enforcement of an injunction

It is not only the obtaining of an injunction which is important but also its enforcement. A major criticism of injunctions granted under the law prior to the 1976 Act was that when it came to enforcement they were not worth the paper on which they were written. If the other party was in breach of the injunction the applicant had to return to court and seek an order for his committal to prison. This procedure was often slow and troublesome (see *post*, p. 72), with the result that it discouraged the battered woman from enforcing her rights (see, for example, Pizzey, *Scream Quietly or the Neighbours will Hear*, Chapter 6). On the recommendation of the Select Committee on Violence in Marriage (para. 45, rec. 17), section 2 of the Act enables a judge to attach a power of arrest to the injunction if:

(1) the injunction contains a provision restraining the other party from using violence against the applicant, or a child living with the applicant or contains an exclusion order, and

(2) the judge is satisfied that the other party has caused actual bodily harm to the applicant or the child concerned, and

(3) the judge considers that he is likely to do so again.

All three conditions must be satisfied (see, for example *McLaren* v. *McLaren* (1978)). The Act again makes it clear that the provisions apply to a man and a woman living together in the same household as husband and wife (s. 2 (2) and see also s. 1 (2) *ante*, p. 58). There are a number of restrictions to note. If the injunction is a non-molestation injuction it must restrain the other party from using violence. If it is not so qualified the judge cannot attach a power of arrest. There is no such qualification if the injunction is an exclusion injunction. A power of arrest is available only against the other party.

If the injunction relates to a child, he must be living with the applicant, and actual bodily harm must have been caused to that particular child by the other party. It is not sufficient for the violence to have been towards any other child. "Actual bodily harm" includes "any hurt or injury calculated to interfere with the health and comfort of the prosecutor" (*R.* v. *Miller* (1954)). This was held to include an hysterical and nervous condition resulting from an assault. Once the requirement of actual bodily harm has been proved, it is to be hoped that the courts will be readily prepared to find a repetition likely. Even if all three conditions can be satisfied there is no guarantee that the judge will attach a power of arrest, for he has a discretion whether or not so to do.

The suggestion from the case of *Lewis* v. *Lewis* (1978) is that a power of arrest is an exceptional remedy. In that case the Court of Appeal considered the possibility of attaching a power of arrest to an injunction granted in divorce proceedings and took the opportunity to discuss some important matters arising from section 2. The Court stressed that a power of arrest is not to be regarded as a routine remedy but is designed for exceptional cases, where for example, there are persistent breaches of an injunction. The Court also stressed the need for giving notice to the other party that a power of arrest is being sought. It felt that the respondent might submit to the injunction but would want strenuously to oppose the attachment of a power of arrest. The need for giving notice is in line with the general rule that when the court is granting and enforcing injunctions in matrimonial proceedings, it should only act *ex parte* (*i.e.* after hearing one side only) in an emergency, when the interests of justice or the protection of the applicant or a child clearly demand immediate intervention by the court (see *Ansah* v. *Ansah* (1977)). Even if the case is an appropriate one for attaching a power of arrest *ex parte*, the power should be limited to the period required to arrange a preliminary hearing *inter partes* (hearing both sides), which would normally be a matter of days. It is therefore unjustifiable and improper to make an injunction *ex parte* "until further order" (see *Ansah* v. *Ansah* (1979), *Morgan* v. *Morgan* (1978) and *post*, p. 70).

As the courts regard the power of arrest as an exceptional remedy, it is to be expected that it will be granted infrequently. This is regrettable if it again means injunctions are not worth the paper on which they are written. Conversely, as suggested in *Lewis* v. *Lewis*, the granting of an injunction might be sufficient in itself.

If a power of arrest is attached, what use is it? This depends upon the willingness of the authorities, *i.e.* the police, to become involved in what may appear to be a purely domestic affair. They have been reluctant to do so in cases of domestic violence. This has been due partly to the embarrassment to them if a prosecution has to be withdrawn because of the woman's later reluctance to give evidence and partly to their fairly well established attitude that the home is beyond their surveillance. Whilst the former point is more relevant to the matter of criminal prosecution (see *post*, p. 73), the latter is very relevant to the question of enforcement of injunctions. The Select Committee on Violence in Marriage recommended that Chief Constables should review their policies on police approach to domestic violence (para. 44, rec. 15) and that each police force should keep statistics about incidents of domestic violence (para. 44, rec. 16).

Section 2 is part of our civil law, not our criminal law. The police are therefore cautious of over-stepping their powers and in some cases are less than helpful (see *Battered Women and Abused Children*, pp. 28, 29). Section 2 (3) provides that, if a power of arrest is attached to an injunction, a constable may arrest, without warrant, a person whom he has reasonable cause for suspecting of being in breach of the injunction by reason of the use of violence or entry into the home. Anyone so arrested must be brought before a judge within 24 hours from the time of the arrest (not counting Christmas Day, Good Friday or any Sunday). During that time, but no longer, the person arrested will be kept in custody, unless a judge has directed that he be released (s. 2 (4) as amended). The police are also under a duty to seek the directions of the court as to the time and place at which that person is to be brought before a judge (s. 2 (5)). By so providing, section 2 makes the enforcement of the civil law part of the role of the police. Their involvement arises, however, only after there has been a breach or suspected breach of the injunction, so the section will not directly affect incidents of initial violence, but by increasing the involvement of the police in domestic disputes, may overcome some of the police reluctance to intervene in such cases. There is a danger, however, that they may see their role as being limited to cases where an injunction has been breached. The police are, to an extent, cast in the role of judge, for upon them falls the burden of deciding whether or not there is an injunction in existence and, if so, whether or not there has been a breach of it. What amounts to "reasonable cause for suspecting" a breach of the injunction? On the former it was suggested (S.C.R., para. 46) that it would be helpful if solicitors sent copies of injunctions to the local police station, so that the police would be aware of the position and more ready to assist in the event of further trouble. The court rules do provide for such copies to be delivered by a court officer to the officer in charge of the police station covering the applicant's address (County Court Rules, Ord. 46, r. 28 (4)). There remains the problem of the mobility of battered women, a problem which can only be solved by some form of centralised registry open for use by any police force. The present system, therefore, has its disadvantages which do not encourage the police in enforcing the injunction. In particular there is the police unfamiliarity with the civil courts and their procedures, which may encourage continued reliance on the criminal law (see *post*, p. 73).

If the injunction is not supported by a power of arrest, the applicant will have to rely on the committal procedure (see *post*, p. 72).

2. *Procedure*

Jurisdiction

To which court is application made? The Act confers powers on the county court (s. 1 (1)), but rules have provided for applications to the High Court (Rules of The Supreme Court (Amendment) Order 1977, R.S.C. Order 90, r. 17). This has not been appreciated in some cases and it has been held that the Act has not enlarged the High Court's jurisdiction (*Crutcher* v. *Crutcher* (1978)). In most cases the appropriate court will be the county court. The relevant rules are the County Court Rules (C.C.R.) which provide that an application under section 1 must be made by originating application to the county court for the district in which either party lives or where the matrimonial home is situated (C.C.R., Ord. 46, r. 28 (2)). Applications are not limited to divorce county courts.

The application should be supported by an affidavit. The normal rule requiring at least 21 clear days' notice is amended to require the giving of at least four days' clear notice (C.C.R., Ord. 46, r. 28 (2A)). An applicant can apply for shorter notice and in emergencies the court can grant an *ex parte* injunction (see *ante*, p. 67 and below). The rules also provide for the hearing to be in chambers (*i.e.* in private) rather than in open court, although the judge has a discretion to hear any particular application in open court (C.C.R., Ord. 46, r. 28 (2B) and see *Practice Direction*, June 24, 1974). This will normally apply only where there is some legal ruling of significance for the future. It should also be remembered (see *ante*, p. 58) that the court only has jurisdiction if the man and woman "are living with each other" (s. 1 (2)). What of the cohabitee who has been driven out? The suggested answer is to read the section as applying to cohabitation up to the time of the acts complained of.

Ex parte injunctions

Reference has already been made to the principle that *ex parte* applications should only be made in an emergency, when the interests of justice or the protection of the applicant or a child clearly demand immediate intervention by the court (see *ante*, p. 67 and *Ansah* v. *Ansah*, C.C.R., Ord. 13, r. 8 (2) (3)). This was confirmed by a *Practice Direction* of June 26, 1978 which states that:

> "An *ex parte* application should not be made, or granted, unless there is real immediate danger of serious injury or irreparable damage. A recent examination of *ex parte* applications shows that nearly 50% were unmeritorious, being made days, or even weeks, after the last incident of which complaint was made."

The Court of Appeal has gone so far as to say that applications by a spouse requiring the other to leave the home should never be *ex parte*, except in the most exceptional circumstances and that such applications are an abuse of the process of the court (*Masich* v. *Masich* (1977)). If an *ex parte* order is made, it must be limited in time to the shortest period necessary to arrange a preliminary hearing *inter partes*. The order must specify the date on which the injunction expires (see *Ansah* v. *Ansah* (1979) and *Morgan* v. *Morgan* (1978)). If it is anticipated that there may be problems serving the order on the other party, it may, exceptionally, be possible that the court will fix a longer period and the order provide that the other party may apply on 24 hours' notice to discharge the injunction.

In conclusion, it can be said that the chances of an *ex parte* injunction being granted are very slim indeed. The courts limit them to extreme cases, and are particularly unlikely to grant them if the injunction sought is one to exclude a party from the home (*Masich*) or where a power of arrest is sought (*Lewis*).

Legal aid and advice

Legal aid and advice are available for applications for an injunction. For details of these schemes see Zander, *Social Workers, their Clients and the Law*, Chap. 2. In urgent cases, for example on application for an *ex parte* injunction, it will be necessary to apply for an emergency certificate.

Power of arrest

The conditions under which a power of arrest will be attached to an injunction and the law relating to the enforcement of that power in the event of a breach of the injunction were discussed earlier (see *ante*, p. 66). The enforcement procedure is also important, for the Court of Appeal has stressed that in cases affecting the liberty of the subject it is essential that orders committing a person to prison for contempt of court should observe the strict legal procedural requirements (*Cinderby* v. *Cinderby*; *Pekesin* v. *Pekesin* (1978)). Moreover, such orders must be correct when made and cannot be subsequently remedied. The appropriate forms must be used (see C.C.R., Ord. 46, r. 28 (3) and (7)) and they must state the evidence, the particular contempt of court of which the other party is guilty and the period for which the other party is committed. (See also *Wellington* v. *Wellington* (1978), and for committal procedure see *post*, p. 72.) The judge before whom a person is brought under section 2 (4) (see *ante*, p. 68) can punish that person for breach of the injunction, notwithstanding that a copy of the injunction has not been served on him and no application for committal has been made according to the rules. (See C.C.R., Ord. 46, r. 28 (6) and *Lewis* v. *Lewis* (1978).)

One can understand the courts' reluctance to deprive a man of his liberty, but when violence sufficient to justify a committal to prison has been proved, it is unfortunate that a woman's protection should be defeated by procedural irregularities. There is evidence of judicial opposition to the Act and some judges will not attach a power of arrest (see *Battered Women and Abused Children*, pp. 29–30, 37–40). It is particularly important, therefore, that the correct procedure is followed. The strict procedural rules call into question the public availability of the law. The system is such that of necessity applicants ought to be legally represented. In the words of one commentator "The hurdles now facing the general practice solicitor are at best a headache, at worst a nightmare" (Robinson, "Domestic Violence: No Ansah" (1979)). Indeed, is this an area of the law with which solicitors are sufficiently conversant to provide the urgent relief needed? Is Legal Aid sufficiently and readily available? If lawyers and judges have difficulty following the procedures what chance does the layman stand? Even with serious social problems of violence it is apparent that the strict legal rules have to be followed if a right is not to be without a remedy.

OTHER REMEDIES

In most cases the appropriate course of action for the battered cohabitee will be to seek an injunction under the 1976 Act. That may not always be possible, for example, if the relationship is not of sufficient stability to satisfy the requirement (s. 1 (2)) that the couple be living together as husband and wife, or if the couple were living together as husband and wife but are doing so no longer (see *ante*, p. 58), or if it is a family cohabitation, or a homosexual cohabitation. The alternative remedies are less than satisfactory (see Freeman, *op. cit.*, Chapter 8). They are to be found in both the civil and criminal law.

1. *The Civil Law*

There remains the pre-1976 Act remedy of an action for damages for assault or trespass to land and claiming an injunction as an ancillary remedy. The chief object of such an action is the obtaining of an injunction, for the amount of damages likely to be awarded in most cases will be small (see *post*, p. 74). Indeed it has been common practice once the injunction has been granted, for the applicant to apply for the hearing of the claim for damages to be adjourned indefinitely. It is essential, however, to sue for damages because an injunction (other than under the 1976 Act) is not a remedy in itself. It is an ancillary remedy, *i.e.* can only be granted in support of a legal right and as such must arise out of a case pending before the court or about to be commenced.

Enforcement of the injunction is by proceedings for committal (or attachment as it is called in the county court) and is only available if the order was properly served and was endorsed with a "penal notice" stating that "unless you obey the directions contained in this order you will be guilty of contempt of court and will be liable to be committed to prison." The courts consider that the real purpose of the committal procedure is to bring the matter back to the court, not with a view to punishing the disobedience but to secure compliance with the order in the future (see *Ansah* v. *Ansah* (1977)). So, committal orders are remedies of last resort and "in family cases they should be the very last resort" (*per* Ormrod L.J. in *Ansah*). If a committal order is made, the person committed to prison may be released by "purging his contempt," *i.e.* by saying he is sorry and will not break the injunction again. There is no minimum period of detention, but courts are reluctant to keep a man in prison for more than a short while on the principle that a short sharp shock is the best remedy. On release the injunction remains in force.

We have seen that a useful alternative to committal is the power, under section 2 of the 1976 Act, to attach a power of arrest to an injunction. It seems that section 2 can be used to attach a power of arrest to an injunction made outside the Act. In *Lewis* v. *Lewis* (1978) the Court of Appeal decided that section 2 was of general application and applies to any case where a judge, either in the High Court or in the county court, grants an injunction in one or more of the forms set out in section 2 (1). In that particular case the proceedings were divorce proceedings, but arguably the same applies in an action for damages, if the injunction complies with section 2 (1) of the 1976 Act (see *ante*, p. 66). There seems no reason to limit the extension to matrimonial proceedings.

Unlike a spouse, a cohabitee cannot seek the protectionary powers of the magistrates' domestic jurisdiction under the Domestic Proceedings and Magistrates' Courts Act 1978. The 1978 Act has not, therefore, followed the lead of the 1976 Act even though it owes much to that Act. The exclusion of cohabitees from the 1978 Act has been attributed first, to the problem of magistrates' courts having to distinguish between couples living in the same household as husband and wife and couples merely living in the same household and, second, to the magistrates' court not being the appropriate forum for determining long-term occupation of the home. The limitation is to be regretted as it denies to cohabitees the quicker and cheaper magistrates' jurisdiction.

A cohabitee cannot use the protectionary powers of the divorce court, there being no marriage which a court can dissolve.

2. *The Criminal Law*

An assault by a cohabitee on his or her partner is, like any other assault, a criminal offence. The victim is therefore entitled to expect the protection of the criminal law either by bringing proceedings himself or by seeking the help of the police. For the most part those expectations have not been realised (compare *R.* v. *Buchanan* (1980) and *R.* v. *McPhillips* (1980)).

A private prosecution can be brought by issuing a summons for assault. The Offences against the Person Act 1861 provides, *inter alia*, for imprisonment on conviction of a "common assault," but a magistrates' court hearing a cohabitee's complaint is unlikely to do more than impose a fine and the complainant will not be granted legal aid. Moreover, this course of action will, at best, do little for the complainant's safety and at worst increase the likelihood of further violence.

As an alternative to a private prosecution, particularly in cases of serious acts of violence, the complainant can seek police help. The reluctance of the police to intervene in a domestic dispute has been discussed in relation to the enforcement of an injunction (see *ante*, p. 68). There is the possibility of their intervention exacerbating the situation. The complainant, realising that the other party will in many cases be released pending the hearing may, for obvious reasons, decline from pursuing the complaint. One survey showed that nearly 99 per cent. of the men responsible for violence against their wives remained at liberty after the police had been informed (see Freeman, *op. cit.*, p. 190 and on the non-enforcement of the criminal law see pp. 184–191).

If the violence complained of amounts to a common assault the police will leave the complainant to pursue his or her own remedy because, generally, proceedings cannot be brought by a police officer (*Nicholson* v. *Booth* (1888), *cf. Pickering* v. *Willoughby* (1907)). Most cohabitees, therefore, will have to institute proceedings themselves. More serious acts of violence may involve other offences, the future of which is discussed in the Criminal Law Revision Committee's Report on Offences Against the Person. First, the violence may amount to assault occasioning actual bodily harm (s. 47), (known as A.B.H.), the meaning of which was discussed earlier (see *R.* v. *Miller* (1954), *ante*, p. 67). An injury to a person's state of mind may be sufficient. Second, it may constitute malicious wounding (s. 20). Wounding means an injury which causes the skin to break (*R.* v. *Wood and McMahon* (1830)) usually stab wounds or cuts, but it is not necessary that any instrument should have been used. So, for example, injuries caused by kicking can amount to wounding (*R.* v. *Duffill* (1843)). Third, bodily harm of a really serious nature constitutes grievous bodily harm (s. 18) (known as G.B.H., see *D.P.P.* v. *Smith* (1960)). Short of homicide the most serious case may constitute attempted murder. In any of these cases the police have a power to arrest. Likewise, if there has been a sexual assault (see Sexual Offences Act 1956 as amended by the Sexual Offences (Amendment) Act 1976) the most serious of which is rape (s. 1). A husband cannot generally be guilty of raping his wife but the same protection does not apply in the case of unmarried partners (see *post*, p. 138).

3. *Compensation for Criminal Violence*

A Report in 1970 called "Reparation by the Offender" (known as The Widgery Report) showed that an offender in a case of criminal violence is rarely sued in the civil courts. This is because of the cost to the victim of bringing civil proceedings compared with the chance of being awarded damages and costs against the offender. It is just not worth it. The Report recommended that remedies should be available in criminal law for compensating the victim of a crime. The recommendation is now incorporated in the Powers of Criminal Courts Act 1973, as amended, which provides for the making of compensation orders against convicted persons. Of the other ways in which the criminal law compensates a victim of crime, only the Criminal Injuries Compensation Scheme is of relevance to problems of domestic violence. It should be regarded as an alternative, not an addition to the compensation order, for where a compensation order has been made, the amount of the order will be deducted from any award of compensation by the Board.

Compensation order

The significance of these orders must not be over-emphasised, for although the Powers of Criminal Courts Act 1973, s. 35 provides that a court which convicts a person, in addition to dealing with him in any other way, may make a compensation order requiring him to pay compensation for any personal injury, loss or damage resulting from the offence or any other offence which is taken into consideration, most compensation orders made by criminal courts are for loss or damage to property and not for personal injury. In determining whether or not to make an order, and if so for how much, the court must have regard to the offender's means so far as they appear or are known to the court. A magistrates' court cannot make a compensation order for more than £1,000 (Criminal Law Act 1977, s. 60 (1)).

Criminal Injuries Compensation Scheme

This Scheme was established in 1964 to make *ex gratia* payments of compensation to, *inter alia*, the victims of violent crime. It is administered by the Criminal Injuries Compensation Board (C.I.C.B.) consisting of legally qualified members. The original Scheme had an important exclusion:

> "Where the victim who suffered injuries and the offender who inflicted them were living together at the time as members of the same family no compensation will be payable. For the purpose of this paragraph where a man and a woman were living together as man and wife they will be treated as if they were married to one another" (para. 7).

Two main reasons were given for the exclusion, first, the difficulty of establishing the facts and, second, the difficulty of ensuring that compensation did not benefit the offender.

In 1978 the report of an interdepartmental working party was published. The working party had reviewed the operation of the C.I.C.B. and made 52 recommendations for changes to the Scheme, including the recommendation that the specific exclusion of applicants who are injured by members of the same family should not be retained (rec. 8). The working party felt that it was unjust that the more seriously injured victims of intra-family violence should be prevented from obtaining compensation under the Scheme.

Nearly all the recommendations of the working party were given effect in a revised Scheme which applies to incidents occurring on and after October 1, 1979. The revised Scheme provides that:

"Where the victim and any person responsible for the injuries which are the subject of the application (whether that person actually inflicted them or not) were living in the same household at the time of the injuries as members of the same family, compensation will be paid only where:

(a) the person responsible has been prosecuted in connection with the offence, except where the Board consider that there are practical, technical or other good reasons why a prosecution has not been brought; and

(b) the injury was one for which compensation. . . . of not less than £500 would be awarded; and

(c) in the case of violence between adults in the family, the Board are satisfied that the person responsible and the applicant stopped living in the same household before the application was made and seem unlikely to live together again; and

(d) in the case of an application under this paragraph by or on behalf of a minor, *i.e.* a person under 18 years of age, the Board are satisfied that it would not be against the minor's interests to make a full or reduced award.

For the purposes of this paragraph, a man and woman living together as husband and wife shall be treated as members of the same family" (para. 8).

If the offence is a sexual offence or one which arose out of a sexual relationship the Board will scrutinise the application with particular care, to see whether there was any responsibility on the part of the victim. Compensation will not be payable unless the Board are satisfied that the offender will not benefit from an award and no compensation will be payable for the maintenance of any child born as a result of a sexual offence (paras. 7 and 10).

The revised Scheme is a clear improvement upon the original, but remains subject to limitations and problems of interpretation, most notably in requiring that the person responsible and the victim stopped "living in the same household" before the application was made. The original Scheme prevented the victim from receiving compensation if she and the person responsible were "living together" at the time as members of the same family. In *R.* v. *Criminal Injuries Compensation Board, ex p. Staten* (1972), it was decided that the original phrase should be given its ordinary meaning and not that which it has in matrimonial law, where the test is that which now appears in the revised Scheme. The change of wording should make it easier to gain compensation, because the fact that two people are living under the same roof does not necessarily mean they are living in the same household, for that requires the sharing of a domestic life (see, for example, *Hopes* v. *Hopes* (1948), *Mouncer* v. *Mouncer* (1972), *Fuller* v. *Fuller* (1973)). Thus, whereas Mr. and Mrs. Staten were "living together" although they slept apart, had no sexual relationship and she did not cook or clean for him, it is very doubtful that they were "living in the same household."

4. *Administrative Remedy*

In addition to any of the remedies discussed so far, if as a result of violence a cohabitee becomes homeless, she may look to the local authority for accommodation (see generally Arden, *Housing: Security and Rent Control*, Chap. 10). This may directly involve the social worker, because a housing authority may well turn to the Social Services Department to investigate the case and make a report. The attitudes of local authorities vary. If the cohabitees are local authority tenants there is a good case for arguing that the tenancy be transferred to the sole name of the battered cohabitee. To do so, some authorities are likely to require legal proceedings to have been taken, in the same way as they used to insist that a wife obtain a magistrates' court's non-cohabitation order before transferring a tenancy to her. It is to be regretted if authorities insist on a cohabitee obtaining an injunction before transferring a tenancy, for where is she to go in the meanwhile, particularly if there is no Women's Aid Centre at hand (see Freeman, *op. cit.*, pp. 167–170)? Even if there is a centre, to seek such aid may relieve the local authority of its duty under the Housing (Homeless Persons) Act 1977.

Under that Act, a duty is placed upon local authorities to house the homeless and those threatened with homelessness. The duty is on the housing authority, which must decide whether or not:
  (a) the applicant is homeless or threatened with homelessness;
  (b) he has a priority need;
  (c) he is intentionally homeless.
A Code of Guidance has been issued which explains how the Act is intended to be applied. Housing authorities are under a duty to have

regard to the Code (s. 12). The Code asks authorities "to respond sympathetically to applications from women who are in fear of violence" (para. 2.10).

A person is homeless if he has no accommodation, or if there is no accommodation which he, together with anyone who normally resides with him as a member of his family, is entitled to occupy (for meaning of "member of the family" see para. 2.8). The definition includes a person who has accommodation but cannot get into it or where it is probable that occupation of it will lead to violence from someone else living in it, or to threats of violence which are likely to be carried out. A person is threatened with homelessness if he is likely to become homeless within 28 days (s. 1).

A person has a priority need if:
  (a) he has dependent children who are living with him or who might reasonably be expected to live with him;
  (b) he is homeless as a result of an emergency (for example, fire, flood or other disaster);
  (c) he or anyone living or reasonably expected to live with him is vulnerable as a result of old age, mental illness or handicap or physical disability or other special reason;
  (d) she is pregnant (s. 2).

Although the Act is designed to include cases of family violence there is no specific provision for battered women, although the Code suggests their inclusion under "other special reason" and says that battered women with children are included (para. 2.12).

Section 17 sets out the circumstances in which a person becomes homeless intentionally, *i.e.* if he deliberately does, or fails to do, something which causes him to become homeless where it would have been reasonable for him to continue in occupation. A person who is unaware of any relevant facts does not become homeless intentionally. The Code says that "a battered woman who has fled the marital home should never be regarded as having become homeless intentionally" (para. 2.16).

Where one member of a family unit, such as a cohabitation, becomes homeless intentionally, the other member remains entitled to apply under the 1977 Act, notwithstanding that the intentionally homeless party might benefit from the application. The housing authority is entitled, however, to look at the conduct of the family as a whole and assume, in the absence of evidence to the contrary, that conduct of one party, which was such that he should be regarded as having become homeless intentionally, was conduct to which the other member of the family was a party (*Lewis* v. *North Devon District Council* (1981)).

Once it has been decided that a person is homeless, has a priority need and is not homeless intentionally, the authority has a duty to secure that accommodation becomes available for his occupation (s. 4 (5)), or if he is threatened with homelessness, to secure that accommodation does not cease to be available (s. 4 (4)). If there is homelessness, or threatened homelessness, but the person does not have a priority need, there is merely a duty to give "advice and appropriate assistance" (s. 4 (2)). If there is homelessness and a priority need but the person became homeless intentionally, there is a duty to secure that accommodation is made available for his occupation until he has had a reasonable opportunity of finding his own (s. 4 (3)) and a duty to give advice and assistance (s. 4 (2)). In the case of intentional threatened homelessness and a priority need the duty is to give advice and assistance (s. 4 (2)).

If a case of possible homelessness comes to the attention of an authority it must make appropriate enquiries, and if the authority has reason to believe that the person may be homeless and have a priority need it must rehouse the person pending any decision (s. 3).

The Code provides that the accommodation should be "reasonably convenient and avoid undue disruption of education, employment or other ties of this kind" (para. 2.1). Even when it has been accepted that there is a duty under s. 4 (5) to secure accommodation, the housing authority can argue there is no local connection with its area. If the authority is of the opinion that neither the applicant, nor anyone to be rehoused with him, has a local connection with the authority's area and that one of them has a local connection with another housing authority's area, where there is no risk of domestic violence, they may notify that authority. If the notified authority agrees with the notification it is then under a duty to secure accommodation. If the notified authority does not so agree, the notifying authority remains responsible until the dispute is settled (s. 5).

If a housing authority is required to secure that accommodation becomes available, it may perform that duty by providing council housing or by seeing that someone else provides accommodation by giving such advice and assistance as to ensure that someone else provides accommodation (s. 6). In so advising the housing authority is not confined to ensuring that the accommodation is obtained from someone else within the housing authority's area (see *R.* v. *Bristol City Council, ex p. Browne* (1979)).

CONCLUSION

This chapter has been concerned with the legal remedies for the problem of violence. The law can, at best, only be a partial remedy, for a battered woman's needs may extend beyond such remedies (see

Freeman, *op. cit.*, Chapter 7); for example, she may need advice, somewhere to go and money to support herself and her children. For advice she may well turn to the Social Services Department, the Citizens' Advice Bureau, Gingerbread or Women's Aid Centre rather than to a lawyer. Immediate accommodation problems may be temporarily solved by seeking refuge at a Women's Aid Centre if one is available, and perhaps, but less likely, the local authority if the woman is classified as homeless for the purposes of the Housing (Homeless Persons) Act 1977 (see above). So far as money is concerned, the battered cohabitee, unlike the battered wife, cannot seek support for herself (as opposed to the children) from her partner and will inevitably look to the State (see Chapter 3).

So far as the legal remedies are concerned, much has been done to improve the lot of battered women, but the law and procedure need simplifying. To this end there is a need for a system of family courts. The many recommendations for a system have so far gone unheeded. Such a system would be as informal as possible and would have a greater chance of emphasising the social problems which lie behind domestic disputes, including cases of domestic violence and provide the necessary welfare and advisory service from social workers, as well as an improved legal service. The courts would exercise both civil and criminal jurisdiction so that the appropriate remedy in each case could be considered within one system, for it must not be forgotten that:

> ". . . what is involved is not the plight of a particular category of unhappy women, but the future of families, involving men, women and—most important of all—their children." (Select Committee on Violence in Marriage, para. 62.)

Further Reading

Bromley, *Family Law* (Butterworths, 5th ed.).
Cretney, *Principles of Family Law* (Sweet and Maxwell, 3rd ed.).
Eekelaar, *Family Law and Social Policy* (Weidenfeld and Nicolson).
Sweet and Maxwell's Family Law Statutes (2nd ed.).
Arden, *Housing: Security and Rent Control* (Sweet and Maxwell).
Battered Women and Abused Children (University of Bradford).
Borland, *Violence in the Family* (Manchester University Press).
Bradley, "Domestic Violence and Matrimonial Proceedings Act 1976" (1978) 41 M.L.R. 592.
Coote and Gill, *Battered Women and the New Law* (Inter-Action and N.C.C.L.).
Criminal Law Revision Committee Fourteenth Report, *Offences Against the Person*, Cmnd. 7844.

Eekelaar and Katz, *Family Violence: An International and Interdisciplinary Study* (Butterworths, Canada).

Freeman, *Violence in the Home* (Saxon House).

Freeman, "The Criminal Injuries Compensation Scheme and The Family—A Comment on the Revised 1979 Scheme" (1980) 10 Fam. Law 37.

Hayes, "Evicting a Spouse from the Matrimonial Home" (1978) 8 Fam. Law 4, 41.

Maidment, "The Law's Response to Marital Violence in England and the U.S.A." (1977) 26 I.C.L.Q. 403.

Maidment, "The Relevance of the Criminal Law to Domestic Violence" (1980) J.S.W.L. 26.

Martin, "Domestic Violence and the Rent Acts" (1978) 128 N.L.J. 154.

Martin, *Violence and the Family* (Wiley).

Migdal, "Domestic Violence—Has the Act Beaten It?" (1979) 9 Fam. Law 136.

Parry, "Somewhere to Live: Excluding the Husband from Occupation of the Matrimonial Home" (1975) 5 Fam. Law 165.

Pizzey, *Scream Quietly or The Neighbours Will Hear* (Penguin).

Report of the Committee on One-Parent Families, Cmnd. 5629.

Report from the Select Committee on Violence in Marriage, Session 1974–75, Vols. I and II (H.C. 553–i, ii).

Report of the Sub-Committee of the Advisory Council on the Penal System, 1970: *Reparation by the Offender* (Home Office).

Review of the Criminal Injuries Compensation Scheme: Report of an Interdepartmental Working Party (H.M.S.O.,1978).

Robinson, "Domestic Violence—A Practitioner's Viewpoint" (1979) 129 N.L.J. 251.

Robinson, "Domestic Violence: No Ansah" (1979) 129 N.L.J. 896.

Sherrin, "Domestic Violence and Proprietary Rights" (1978) 8 Fam. Law 176.

5 Death

THE DECEASED'S ESTATE

There is a general rule in English law of freedom of testation, *i.e.* when you die you can leave what you like to whomsoever you like. To achieve this, it is of course essential to make a will (on making a will see Zander, *Social Workers, their Clients and the Law*, Chap. 11).

1. *Will*

If the deceased made a valid will (*i.e.* died "testate"), the property forming his estate will be disposed of in accordance with the terms of the will.

A testator who wishes to leave property to a specific person should identify that person by name, rather than by status. A gift in a will to "my wife" or "my husband" will, in the absence of contrary evidence, be taken to mean the person to whom the deceased was married at the date of the will (*Re Coley* (1903)).

Cases have occurred where such a gift has been intended not for a spouse but for a cohabitee. It is possible for the prima facie meaning to be overridden in the context of the particular gift, even to the extent that a person who was not married to the deceased has been held entitled to benefit. It is essential, however, that the testator has made it clear that he is describing that particular person. So, in *Re Brown* (1910) the testator, a widower, left a legacy to "my wife" and the court decided that the woman with whom the testator lived, but to whom he was not married, was entitled to the legacy. It is not essential, therefore, for the testator to have named the person, but his intention will be that much clearer if he has done so. Each case will depend upon the construction of the particular will in the light of the particular circumstances. In *Re Smalley* (1929) a testator by his will left all his property to "my wife E.A.S." At his death he was survived by a wife M.A.S. and by a woman E.A.M., with whom he had contracted a later, bigamous marriage and who lived with him as his wife. E.A.M. was known as E.A.S. and believed she was his wife. The Court of Appeal held that the testator intended to benefit E.A.M. and she was entitled to his property.

Similarly in *Re Lynch* (1943) the testator, a widower, appointed "my wife Annie Ethel Lynch" one of his executors and left part of his estate "to my wife during her widowhood." The parties were not married and could not marry because they were within the prohibited degrees of relationship (see *ante*, p. 7). They had cohabited as man and wife for five years and represented themselves as man and wife. The court decided that on the construction of the will the testator had provided his own dictionary and when he referred to "my wife" he intended Annie Ethel Lynch, so she was entitled to benefit. In view of the increase in the incidence of cohabitation, the chance of cases of the kind just discussed arising must also increase. Hence the need for the testator to identify clearly the beneficiary.

If cohabitees marry the marriage will automatically revoke any existing will of either party (Wills Act 1837, s. 18), unless the will expressly states that it was made in contemplation of that particular marriage, in which case the will is not revoked (Law of Property Act 1925, s. 177). A will is not revoked by divorce or by cohabitation.

It is important to realise that a witness who attests a will is disqualified from benefiting under the will, as is the spouse of any such witness (Wills Act 1837, s. 15). The rule does not apply to the cohabitee of a witness.

2. *Intestacy*

If a person dies without having made a valid will (*i.e.* dies "intestate") his estate will be disposed of according to the rules of intestate succession (Administration of Estates Act 1925, s. 46 as amended). The importance of making a will in order to benefit a cohabitee is illustrated by the rules of intestate succession, for whereas on the death of a spouse intestate the surviving spouse has rights of inheritance from the deceased's estate, not so a surviving cohabitee on the death of a partner.

A surviving spouse has a right on intestacy to the deceased's personal chattels (*i.e.* personal belongings other than goods used for business purposes and money or securities for money, 1925 Act, s. 55) and to a statutory legacy, the amount of which depends upon the existence of other relatives of the deceased. If there are no children, no parents, brothers, sisters, or children of any brothers or sisters, the surviving spouse receives the whole estate. If there are children the spouse's statutory legacy is the first £40,000 and a life interest (*i.e.* entitlement to the property during the recipient's lifetime but normally only to the income not the capital) in half the rest of the estate, the other half going to the children, who also get the half share of the surviving spouse on his or her death. If there are no children, but a parent, brother, sister or children of a brother or sister, the surviving spouse's legacy is increased to £85,000 and an absolute interest (not a life interest) in half the rest, the other half going to the parent or equally to the parents if more than one, if both are dead then equally between the brothers and sisters. The result of these complex rules is that in most cases the surviving spouse inherits the whole estate.

If the deceased's estate includes a house in which the surviving spouse was living at the date of the deceased's death, the surviving spouse may require the house to be transferred to him, or her, in, or towards, satisfaction of his or her entitlement to the deceased's estate (Intestates' Estates Act 1952, s. 5 and Sched. 2).

On the intestate death of a cohabitee, the surviving cohabitee inherits nothing. The deceased's estate, in the absence of a surviving spouse, will be held on trust for the deceased's children (see *post*, p. 122). In the absence of children the estate will pass to the parents (in equal shares if both survive), and in the absence of children and parents to the following relatives in order, brothers and sisters, grandparents, uncles and aunts.

The only circumstances in which a surviving cohabitee could benefit is if there is no one to inherit, in which case the estate passes to the Crown and the Crown has a discretion to make payments for dependants and "other persons for whom the intestate might reasonably have been expected to make provision" (Administration of Estates Act 1925, s. 46 (1) (vi)). This could include a cohabitee, although a claim is more likely under the Inheritance (Provision for Family and Dependants) Act 1975, for any property which passes to the Crown is subject to claims under that Act (s. 24). So far as intestate succession is concerned, it is therefore to a cohabitee's benefit to marry a partner.

3. *Claim for Financial Provision*

A claim against the deceased's estate, including a claim by a cohabitee, may be possible under the Inheritance (Provision for Family and Dependants) Act 1975, notwithstanding the rules of testate and intestate succession.

Who can apply?

Cohabitees can claim under the 1975 Act on the death of a partner on the ground that the deceased's will and/or the law of intestacy do not "make reasonable financial provision for the applicant" (s. 1 (1)). The Act, which implemented the recommendations of the Law Commission

(Law Com. No. 61), applies only if the deceased died domiciled (see *post*, p. 141) in England and Wales (s. 1 (1)). The place of death is irrelevant.

Before the 1975 Act claims under earlier legislation were limited to members of the deceased's family. The qualified applicants now include "any person ... who immediately before the death of the deceased was being maintained, either wholly or partly, by the deceased" (s. 1 (1) (*e*)). Other qualified applicants, *i.e.* a spouse, a former spouse who has not remarried, a child (including an illegitimate child, see *post*, p. 123) or anyone treated by the deceased as a child of the family are defined by reference to a family relationship. The extension to a relationship defined in terms of dependency was designed to include cases where failure to provide was accidental or unintentional. "In these cases an order for family provision would be doing for the deceased what he might reasonably be assumed to have wished to do himself. This argument carries particular weight when the 'dependant' is a person with whom the deceased has been cohabiting" (Law Com. No. 61, para. 90).

It is noticeable, however, that a financial duty is recognised on death but not during the parties' lifetime (see Chapter 3). Is it right that dependence should be acknowledged only after death? Is there not a need for a comprehensive review of the basis on which support rights and obligations between cohabitees are recognised (see Chapter 9)?

In what circumstances is an applicant regarded as "being maintained, either wholly or partly, by the deceased"? The answer, in the words of the Act, is "if the deceased, otherwise than for full valuable consideration, was making a substantial contribution in money or money's worth towards the reasonable needs of that person" (s. 1 (3)). In short, the applicant must have been largely financially dependent upon the deceased (see, for example, *Re Wilkinson* (1978), *Jelley* v. *Iliffe* (1980)) and have been so at the deceased's death (s. 1 (1) (*e*)). It is not sufficient if the parties merely shared their lives and equally contributed to the maintenance of each other (see, for example, *Re Beaumont* 1980)). Likewise if the surviving cohabitee maintained the deceased, the survivor has no claim against the deceased, however meritorious such a claim might be.

The fundamental issue, therefore, for any applicant is the extent of the financial dependency on the deceased; the greater the dependency the greater the chances of success. If the relationship between the applicant and the deceased is one of housekeeper and employer, dependency will be very difficult for the applicant to prove, whereas there will be a stronger claim in the case of a stable cohabitation where the parties have lived together as man and wife, rather than as employer and employee.

The case of *C.A.* v. *C.C.* (1978) illustrates the distinction. An 18-year-old girl who had an illegitimate daughter went to live with a divorced man who was seeking a housekeeper. He made it clear that they would live as husband and wife and he bought her a wedding ring. They remained unmarried. The girl received no wages but was given housekeeping money. The man insisted that the girl's baby be given for adoption because he did not wish to bring up another man's child. They later had an illegitimate son themselves. Before the relationship the man had made a will leaving all his property to his legitimate son by his former wife. He discussed making a new will but he died without doing so. The will therefore remained in force, for whereas marriage revokes a will, cohabitation does not (see *ante*, p. 83). The girl received nothing under the will and she applied under the 1975 Act. It was argued against her that she did not qualify under the Act because she had gone to the deceased as housekeeper and had got a good bargain. The argument was rejected, because she and the deceased had had a stable affectionate relationship and the facts indicated a family. She was a *de facto* wife. The deceased's estate therefore had to provide for her and their child as well as his legitimate son.

The result seems just. It has been argued that to allow a "mistress" to claim is a retrograde step, but in reply it can be said that the Act caters for partners to a stable relationship and that a moral duty is owed to the surviving partner of such a relationship. The Act is hardly thereby becoming a "mistresses' charter."

The discussion so far has related to claims by a cohabitee against the deceased's estate. If a deceased cohabitee has provided for his partner in his will, but has not adequately provided for his spouse, then the surviving spouse can seek an order that some part of the estate be given for his or her benefit (for kinds of provision, see *post*, p. 87); likewise, if inadequate provision has been made by the deceased for a former spouse (see below) or for any child (see *ante*, p. 85), or for a second mistress (see, for example, *Malone* v. *Harrison* (1979)).

The outcome of any claim by a surviving spouse will depend upon the reasonableness of the deceased's failure to provide for his marriage partner. It may be, for example, that the estate is too small to provide for both his spouse and his cohabitee and so a choice has to be made between the moral obligation to the cohabitee and the legal obligation to the spouse. Thus, if the spouse has adequate means whereas the cohabitee is destitute, it will be reasonable for there to be no provision for the surviving spouse. Even before the 1975 Act the courts recognised that in such circumstances the deceased's moral obligation to a cohabitee may defeat a widow's application (*Re Joslin* (1941)). It may be, however, that in many cases the deceased also had a moral obligation to the spouse if they had lived together for a lengthy period before the deceased's cohabitation with someone else began. Moreover the Act provides for a higher standard of financial provision for spouses than for cohabitees (see below), so if a cohabitee is self-supporting her chances of successfully claiming against the claims of a spouse cannot be strong.

An application can be made by a former spouse of the deceased, for example where the marriage ended in divorce, provided that the applicant spouse has not remarried (s. 1 (1) (*b*)). A former spouse who has remarried may still be able to claim under s. 1 (1) (*e*) if he or she was wholly or partly dependent on the deceased at the date of his death. A former spouse's claim is limited to maintenance. On the granting of a decree of divorce, nullity or judicial separation or at any time thereafter, the parties can agree that neither of them shall be entitled, on the other's death, to apply for financial provision. The court must give its approval to any such agreement and embody the agreement in the court order (s. 15). A cohabitee who has an ex-spouse in respect of whom such an order is in force, will be able to leave his property free from any claims under the 1975 Act by the former spouse.

Reasonable financial provision

Once a person has shown that he is qualified to apply, he must then show that the deceased has failed to make reasonable financial provision for him. What is reasonable financial provision? There is here an important distinction. If the applicant is a spouse, reasonable financial provision means such financial provision as it would be reasonable in all the circumstances to receive, whether or not for the applicant's maintenance. In the case of any other applicant, including a cohabitee, reasonable financial provision is limited to maintenance (s. 1 (2)). A spouse is treated as though the marriage had ended by divorce (s. 3 (2) and see *post*, p. 89) and therefore is entitled to be considered for a share of the deceased's capital, but a cohabitee can look only for maintenance.

Maintenance in favour of a cohabitee can take the form of a lump sum (see, for example, *Malone* v. *Harrison* (1979)). In *C.A.* v. *C.C.*, discussed earlier (see *ante*, p. 86) the net value of the estate was between £25,000 and £35,000 of which the court awarded the cohabitee applicant £5,000, the remainder of the estate being divided between the two boys.

The principles to be applied in deciding whether or not reasonable financial provision has been made for the applicant were considered by the Court of Appeal in *Re Coventry* (1979). The Court of Appeal emphasised that each case depends upon its own facts, but that it is not sufficient that the applicant is in financial need, for that fact alone will not necessarily make it unreasonable that no financial provision has been made for the applicant. The court, in deciding whether or not reasonable financial provision has been made, has to make a value judgment. It is not a question of the court deciding how the deceased's assets should be fairly divided, nor is it a question of whether it might have been reasonable for the deceased to have provided for the applicant, but whether in all the circumstances, looked at objectively, it is unreasonable that the deceased's estate does not so provide.

It is only when the applicant has shown that the deceased's estate has failed to make reasonable financial provision that the court can proceed to decide how, if at all, to exercise its powers under the 1975 Act.

Considerations when deciding a claim

Section 3 sets out the matters which the court must consider in deciding first whether or not reasonable financial provision has been made for the applicant's maintenance and, second, if such provision has not been made, what order, if any, should be made. These matters, which are the same for both considerations, are the financial resources and financial needs which the applicant, any other applicant, or any beneficiary of the deceased's estate, has or is likely to have in the foreseeable future; any obligations which the deceased had towards any applicant or beneficiary; the size and nature of the estate; any physical or mental disability of an applicant or beneficiary and any other matter, including the conduct of the applicant or anyone else, which the court may consider relevant (s. 3 (1)). In addition in the case of an application by a cohabitee, the court must consider the extent to which, and the basis upon which, the deceased assumed responsibility for the applicant's maintenance and the length of time he maintained the applicant (s. 3 (4) and see *Re Beaumont* (1980), where the need to show that the deceased had assumed responsibility for the applicant was seen as a pre-condition to the making of an application).

In considering the matters to which the court is required to have regard, it is the facts as known at the date of the hearing which are material (s. 3 (5) and see the pre-Act case of *Lusternick* v. *Lusternick* (1972)). So the court can take into account any change of circumstances after the deceased's death, for example, the fact that the applicant is being maintained by someone else. When the court is deciding whether or not the deceased's estate makes reasonable financial provision for the applicant, the test is an objective one, *i.e.* in the light of the circumstances as viewed by the court at the date of the hearing and not as viewed by the deceased at the time of his death (see, for example, *Re Goodwin* (1968) and *Re Shanahan* (1971)).

When considering section 3, as any potential applicant should, the size of the deceased's estate is clearly an important factor and in the case of small estates the cost of litigation may well make a claim unprofitable (see, for example, *Re Clayton* (1966), *Re Coventry* (1979)). This point is important for social workers to bear in mind, for many of their clients will have neither large estates, nor claims in respect of large estates. The court will have to take into account the alternative sources of income which are available to a surviving cohabitee, for example, supplementary benefit. Likewise the income of any beneficiaries of the estate must be considered, for the amount the beneficiaries will receive will be reduced by any order under the Act.

Competing claims are particularly likely where, for example, a husband and wife separate, the husband cohabits with another woman then he dies without making provision for his cohabitee. If she applies under the Act the court, in balancing the competing claims, will consider *inter alia* the income and capital of the applicant and the wife as well as any other beneficiary, together with their financial obligations and responsibilities (s. 3 (6)). The length of the cohabitation and the marriage, the age of the parties and their contribution to the welfare of the families are not specifically referred to, as they are on an application by a spouse or former spouse (s. 3 (2)), but are likely to be relevant as "any other matter" (s. 3 (1) (*g*)). The deceased's reasons for his dispositions are not a factor to which the court's attention is specifically directed as they were under earlier legislation, but they too can be, and are being, considered as "any other matter."

Specific statutory reference is made to the conduct of the applicant or any other person, so in the above example the conduct of both the surviving cohabitee and wife could be relevant. If the approach suggested by the Law Commission (Law Com. No. 61, paras. 35 &36) is the accepted one, the court will limit conduct to that which is "obvious and gross" (see *post*, p. 128), at least on the application of a surviving spouse. It is submitted that the test to be applied on the application of a surviving cohabitee should be the same.

Type of order

Having considered the matters set out in section 3, the court may then make one or more of the orders in section 2. An order in favour of a cohabitee can only be for his or her maintenance (see *ante*, p. 87) but can take the form of periodical payments, a lump sum (in one or more instalments, s. 7), transfer or settlement of property, or purchase and transfer or settlement of property (see, for example, *Re Haig* (1979)).

An order can only be made out of the deceased's net estate (s. 8 (1)), *i.e.* generally all property of which the deceased had power to dispose less funeral and other expenses, debts and liabilities, including any capital transfer tax payable (see further s. 25 (1)). If the deceased was a joint tenant of property (see *ante*, p. 12 and *post*, p. 92), the court can order that the deceased's share be treated as part of his estate rather than pass to the surviving joint tenant (s. 9). So, for example, a surviving spouse's right of survivorship (see *post*, p. 92) in the home could be subject to a claim by a cohabitee.

The deceased's estate may also include property disposed of during his lifetime with the intention of defeating an application for financial provision (s. 10). If certain conditions are satisfied the person who received the benefit of the disposition (the donee) may be ordered to provide money or property up to the value he received, for the purpose of providing financial provision, irrespective of whether or not the donee still has any of the property given to him. The court also has power to review contracts made with the intention of defeating an application for financial provision (s. 11).

An order for financial provision operates retrospectively from the date of the deceased's death (s. 19). This may affect liability for capital transfer tax, for if an order is made in favour of a cohabitee at the expense of a surviving spouse, the exemption from capital transfer tax in favour of spouses will not operate (see *ante*, p. 54). Conversely if an order is made in favour of a surviving spouse at the expense of a cohabitee, the exemption will apply.

Procedure

The county court has jurisdiction where the deceased's net estate is less than £15,000 (s. 22 as amended). If the estate exceeds that amount the appropriate court is the High Court, either the Chancery Division or the Family Division. The Law Commission's recommendation that the High Court jurisdiction should be assigned exclusively to the Family Division (Law Com. No. 61, rec. 63) has not been implemented. This is to be regretted, for surely matters of a family nature should be dealt with in the Family Division, or even better a family court (see *ante*, p. 80).

An application must be made within six months from the date on which representation (*i.e.* probate or letters of administration) to the deceased's estate was first taken out, unless the court gives permission for a later application (s. 4, see for example *Re Ruttie* (1969)). An order under section 9 in relation to property of which the deceased was joint owner (*i.e.* as "joint tenant") can only be made if the application was made within the six months' period. A time limit is imposed so that after it has expired the personal representatives can distribute the estate and so that a joint tenant does not have to wait indefinitely to discover if he is going to be deprived of the property. The personal representatives are not liable for having distributed the estate after the six months' period, but property may be recovered from the beneficiaries to whom it has been distributed (s. 20 (1)).

If an applicant is in immediate need of financial help, the court has power to make an interim order (s. 5 and see *Re Ralphs* (1968)).

THE HOME

One of the questions that a surviving cohabitee may ask a social worker is, "What rights do I have over the home?" The answer will depend upon the type of occupation, (see Arden, *Housing: Security and Rent Control*, Chapter 2) in particular whether the home was owned or rented by one or both of the parties.

1. *Owned*

If the home was owned solely by the deceased cohabitee, then it will be disposed of according to the deceased's will, or if there is no valid will, according to the law of intestacy. The surviving cohabitee will succeed to the home only if it is left to him or her in the will, or if the survivor can establish a beneficial interest in the property (see *ante*, p. 14), for a cohabitee has no rights of succession on a partner's intestacy (see *ante*, p. 84). If the property is left to the surviving cohabitee it might still be subject to a claim by a spouse or former spouse of the deceased, particularly if the property is the former matrimonial home, either on the ground that the surviving spouse has a beneficial interest in the property or under the Inheritance (Provision for Family and Dependants) Act 1975 (see above).

If the home was owned solely by the surviving cohabitee, ownership will remain unchanged, unless it can be shown that the deceased had a beneficial interest in the property, or unless the property had formerly belonged to the deceased and had been conveyed to the surviving cohabitee as a means of defeating a claim by a third party, for example, a member of the deceased's family under the Inheritance (Provision for Family and Dependants) Act 1975 (see s. 10 *ante*, p. 90), or a creditor (Law of Property Act 1925, s. 172; Bankruptcy Act 1914, s. 42). If the home was jointly owned by the deceased and the surviving cohabitee, the succession rights depend upon the nature of the joint ownership (see Chapter 2). If the property was owned by the parties as "joint tenants," then on the death of one, the survivor automatically inherits the other's share. This right of survivorship between joint tenants, which is known as *jus accrescendi*, is subject to claims against the deceased's share under the Inheritance (Provision for Family and Dependants) Act 1975 (see s. 9 *ante*, p. 90). The right of survivorship does not operate if either of the parties has "severed" the joint tenancy during their lifetime (see *ante*, p. 13). If the joint tenancy is severed the parties then own the property as "tenants in common."

If the property was owned by the parties as tenants in common, each is regarded as owning a separate share, so on the death of one of the parties his share forms part of his estate and does not pass automatically to the survivor.

It is thus vital, when any couple, whether married or unmarried, buy property jointly, that their intentions in the event of the death of either of them are made clear in the title documents and legal advice should be sought accordingly.

2. *Rented*

If the home was rented by the deceased cohabitee alone and the tenancy was a protected one under the Rent Act 1977 (see further Arden, *op. cit.*, Chapter 4), the surviving cohabitee may be able to continue in occupation and hence become a "statutory tenant by succession." The 1977 Act provides that if the tenant dies leaving no surviving spouse (see *post*, p. 94), but a member of his family was residing with him at the time of death and for the six months up to his death, that person shall be the statutory tenant if, and so long as, he occupies the dwelling-house as his residence (Sched. 1, para. 3).

A cohabitee can, in certain circumstances, be a member of the tenant's family for this purpose. The law in this respect reflects a post-war change in social attitudes. It had been accepted that if an unmarried couple had a child they could be said to be living as a family (*Hawes* v. *Evenden* (1953)) but not otherwise (*Gammans* v. *Ekins* (1950)). A different approach was adopted in the important case of *Dyson Holdings Ltd.* v. *Fox* (1975).

In the *Dyson* case Jack Wright and Olive Fox lived together as man and wife for 40 years and were known as Mr. and Mrs. Wright. In 1940 they moved into rented property of which Mr. Wright was tenant. He died in 1961 and Mrs. Wright continued to pay the rent. In 1973 the landlord discovered that Mrs. Wright was not Mr. Wright's widow. Had she been his widow she would have had the protection of the Rent Act (see *post*, p. 94). As she was not, the landlord brought proceedings for possession on the ground that she was not a member of the tenant's family and was thus a trespasser. The county court judge ordered her out of the house. She appealed to the Court of Appeal where it was held that the meaning of the word "family" had changed with the passage of time and people generally would have included Mrs. Wright as a member of Mr. Wright's family.

The *Dyson* case does not mean that all cohabitees will be regarded as a member of their partner's family. If the relationship is only casual or intermittent it will not be classified as a family unit. "Family" means more than household. There can be great difficulties in deciding whether or not the relationship is of sufficient stability to amount to a family and it is questionable whether or not a court is the appropriate body for undertaking such an investigation. Certainly it is not a matter on which a social worker could advise with any great confidence, particularly in view of the courts' later reluctance to follow the *Dyson* decision.

The case of *Helby* v. *Rafferty* (1978) illustrates a relationship which the court found to be of insufficient permanence and stability to justify the parties being regarded as members of a family. Miss Taylor was the tenant of a flat. In 1972, Mr. Rafferty, her lover, moved into the flat and they lived together thereafter. In 1974 she became ill and he looked after her and nursed her until her death in 1977, after which he continued living in the flat. The landlord brought an action against him for possession. Mr. Rafferty argued that the landlord was not entitled to possession because at the date of Miss Taylor's death he had been a member of her family. The Court of Appeal decided he had not been, having regard in particular to the fact that she had not adopted the character of a wife and they had not represented themselves to the world as man and wife. The relationship was thus regarded by the court as different from that in the *Dyson* case. The decision is open to the criticism that it encourages false pretences, *i.e.* a couple will have a better chance of being regarded as a family if they hold themselves out as husband and wife. Also, the Court of Appeal doubted the validity of giving the word "family" a different interpretation from time to time and expressed concern as to how the courts are to determine the popular meaning of a word.

It is noteworthy that in the four cases discussed the women claimants were successful (in *Hawes* and *Dyson*), whilst the men claimants were not (in *Gammans* and *Helby*). The inference arising, that it is acceptable to regard a female but not a male cohabitee as a member of the other cohabitee's family, is not supported by the Court of Appeal decision in *Watson* v. *Lucas* (1980). In that case Mr. Lucas, a married man, chose not to divorce his wife before living in a permanent and stable relationship with a Mrs. Sullivan. They lived together as husband and wife for nearly 20 years up to her death, in the flat of which she was the protected tenant. On her death, the landlord, Mrs. Watson, gave Mr. Lucas notice to quit. He claimed that he was entitled to stay in the flat as a member of Mrs. Sullivan's family. Their relationship had been that of a married couple except that they retained their own names. The Court of Appeal decided, by a majority, that an association which had every outward appearance of marriage, except the false pretence of being a marriage, constituted a family. If the relationship looked like a marriage in the sense of a life-long union with nothing casual or temporary about it, it was a family until the House of Lords decided that *Dyson* was wrongly decided. Moreover, a man can have more than one family, although he would have difficulty in residing with more than one and it would be impossible so to reside to succeed to a protected tenancy. The dissenting judge thought that the case differed from *Dyson* in three respects. First, the woman had been the tenant, second, the parties conveyed the impression that the relationship was extra-marital and third, the man was married. He considered the second and third to be relevant, but not the first. The court granted leave to appeal to the House of Lords so the matter may not yet be settled. It is submitted that the majority decision is correct. The important issue is the nature of the relationship, not which party is tenant, not whether they have masqueraded as husband and wife and not the fact that either party is already married.

The meaning of the term "family" has already been considered by the House of Lords in *Carega Properties* v. *Sharratt* (1979) in relation to a cohabitation of a platonic nature between a man and a childless widow, 50 years his senior. It was decided that two adults who lived together in a platonic relationship could not, in the absence of any other relationship, be a family for the purpose of the Rent Act (see also *Ross* v. *Collins* (1964)). There must be a relationship by blood, marriage, adoption or regular sexual intercourse.

It seems that the following types of cohabitation will constitute a family for the purpose of the Rent Act: brother and sister (*Price* v. *Gould* (1930)); parent and child (including illegitimate children, step-children and adopted children, whether or not there has been a legal adoption (*Brock* v. *Wollams* (1949)) so presumably also foster children) and in-laws living together (*Standingford* v. *Probert* (1949)). As we have seen, an unrelated couple living together as man and wife may be included, particularly if they have children or if the relationship has been a permanent and stable one involving regular sexual intercourse. A homosexual cohabitation does not constitute a family.

The position of a surviving spouse is far more certain. The Rent Act 1977 originally provided for the tenant's widow to succeed to the tenancy if, and so long as, she occupied the dwelling-house as her residence and provided that she was residing with him at his death

(Sched. 1, para. 2). There was no express reference to a tenant's widower, although he was included as "a member of the original tenant's family" under paragraph 3 (see *Salter* v. *Lask* (1925)). The Housing Act 1980 extends the provision in favour of widows to any surviving spouse residing in the dwelling-house immediately before the death of the deceased (s. 76).

A surviving cohabitee who is a member of the tenant's family, is in a less favourable position than a surviving spouse, because in addition to residing with the tenant at the time of death, he must have done so for the preceding six months. Moreover, if there was more than one member of the tenant's family so living, they have to agree amongst themselves who will be the new tenant. If they cannot agree the court will decide.

A tenancy can pass in this way, at most, twice, and only then if the first successor was still a statutory tenant, *i.e.* was still living in the house immediately before his death and died leaving a spouse residing with him at his death or, if no spouse, if there was a member of the first successor's family residing with him at his death and for the previous six months (Sched. 1, paras. 5–7 as amended by Housing Act 1980). On the second successor's death the landlord is entitled to claim possession.

The discussion so far has related to a home rented by the deceased cohabitee alone. If the tenancy was in the surviving cohabitee's name, his or her rights are unaffected. If the tenancy was a joint one, with the surviving cohabitee, the tenancy will continue in favour of the survivor.

Security of tenure and succession on the death of the tenant have been extended by the Housing Act 1980 to local authority tenancies (ss. 28 and 30). A person is qualified to succeed if he is the tenant's spouse and occupied the dwelling-house as his only or main home at the tenant's death. If there is no spouse, another member of the tenant's family, who has occupied the house as his only or main home for the year before the tenant's death, may succeed. If there is more than one member of the tenant's family they must agree between them. Where there is no such agreement the landlord may select.

PENSIONS AND STATE BENEFITS

1. *Pension Funds*

Many pension funds provide for payment to the deceased's widow (and sometimes widower) but not to a surviving cohabitee. In all cases it is necessary to look at the provisions of the scheme concerned. So, for example, some provide for payment to the person nominated by the deceased, which could include a cohabitee. Others make provision for payment to a "dependent relative" in the absence of a surviving spouse, but such payments are often at the discretion of the pension fund. Moreover, a cohabitee (other than in a family cohabitation) will be unlikely to come within the scheme's definition of a relative. If the scheme provides for payment to a "dependant," it will depend upon the scheme's definition as to whether or not a cohabitee is included; for example, a definition that "dependants means persons who in the opinion of the trustees shall have been wholly or partly maintained or financially assisted by the member" may well include a cohabitee, whereas a definition based on that in the Fatal Accidents Act 1976 (see *post*, p. 97) would not.

A surviving spouse in receipt of a pension should note that some schemes provide for the pension to be payable until death, marriage, or living with another as man and wife. So, not only may a surviving cohabitee receive no pension, but also a surviving spouse who becomes a cohabitee may lose one.

Similarly any war pension payable in favour of a widow of a member of the armed forces, who died as a result of service in those forces after September 2, 1939, stops if she cohabits with a man as his wife (Royal Warrant, September 19, 1964, Cmnd. 2467, art. 42 (1)), but may be restored if the cohabitation stops (art. 42 (6)). If there is no widow, a pension may be payable to a woman who was living with the deceased as his wife and who has a child of his in her care, for which she is receiving an allowance (art. 30 (1)).

2. *Widow's Benefit*

It was seen in Chapter 3 that cohabitees acquire no national insurance pension rights as a result of their partner's contributions. So a surviving cohabitee is not entitled to a widow's allowance, a widowed mother's allowance or a widow's pension, for "widow" is limited to a woman who has lost a husband by death. The social security legislation makes no provision for the extension of the term to include those who were living together as husband and wife at the time of the man's death. It is ironic, therefore, that the legislation should deprive a widow of benefit for any period during which "she and a man to whom she is not married are living together as husband and wife" (Social Security Act 1975, ss. 24 (2), 25 (3) and 26 (3) as amended by Social Security (Miscellaneous Provisions) Act 1977, s. 22 (2)). It has been argued that the sum saved by this disqualification on account of cohabitation does not justify the distress caused, at a time of emotional upset, by the suggestion of cohabitation (see Calvert, *Social Security Law*, pp. 233–234).

3. *Death Grant*

Death grant is not payable on the strength of a cohabiting partner's national insurance contributions. Death grant is payable *inter alia* where the deceased was a qualifying contributor or the deceased was, at death, the husband, wife, widower or widow of a qualifying contributor (Social Security Act 1975, s. 32 and Sched. 3, para. 7). So a cohabitee cannot rely on his or her contributions to claim a grant on the death of the other partner.

As discussed in Chapter 3, one is left with the impression that with regard to State benefits and cohabitation there is little coherence or consistency in the relevant sections, save that in so far as cohabitation is recognised it is so as to deny benefit.

COMPENSATION FOR DEATH

If a cohabitee is killed in an accident as a result of another's negligence, then the surviving cohabitee, unlike a surviving spouse, cannot bring an action for compensation under the Fatal Accidents Act 1976. The 1976 Act limits actions to "dependants," *i.e.* a wife, husband, parent, grandparent, child, grandchild, brother, sister, uncle, aunt or issue of the last four. Parties to a non-family cohabitation are therefore excluded, but any children of the relationship can bring an action and they may also recover for loss of payment by the deceased partner to the surviving parent which was for their benefit (see *K. v. J.M.P. Co. Ltd.* (1975)).

An action under the 1976 Act is brought by "dependants" to compensate them for their loss of financial support by the deceased. In addition there is the possibility of an action against the negligent party by the deceased's estate under the Law Reform (Miscellaneous Provisions) Act 1934 for damages for the deceased's loss of expectation of life. Any damages so recovered, which would not be large, would go to the deceased's estate and could benefit a cohabitee who stands to inherit from, or has a claim against, the deceased's estate.

If the deceased died as a result of criminal injuries coming within the Criminal Injuries Compensation Scheme, a spouse or dependant may seek compensation under the Scheme. For this purpose compensation is payable to any person entitled to claim under the Fatal Accidents Act 1976 and thus not to a cohabitee. The Scheme provides that "spouse" does not include "so-called common-law wives" (para. 15). Children of the deceased can apply.

If the deceased died as a result of injuries caused by an accident in the course of his work, certain people may be entitled to industrial death benefits (Social Security Act 1975, ss. 50 (2) (*c*), 67–75). Usually this will be the deceased's widow, but others may be entitled to benefit, namely, a widower, children, parents, relatives and a woman having care of the deceased's children. No provision is made for unmarried persons living as husband and wife. If at the date of the accident and for the period between the accident and the death, the deceased had a family which included any children; and a woman was living with the deceased, had care of the children and was wholly or mainly maintained by the deceased, she is entitled to benefit. Although intended to benefit "housekeepers" (see *ante*, p. 53) the term could include a cohabitee who was financially dependent on the deceased and who looked after the deceased's children.

Any industrial death benefit payable to a widow is suspended while she is "living as husband and wife with a man not her husband" (1975 Act, s. 67 (2) as amended by Social Security (Miscellaneous Provisions) Act 1977, s. 22 (4)). There is no corresponding provision in respect of widower's benefit. Similarly any benefit payable to the deceased's mother (but not father), is suspended during any such cohabitation by her, unless she was so living immediately before the deceased's death (1975 Act, s. 71 (3) as amended). Female relatives and a woman caring for the deceased's children likewise lose benefit whilst living as husband and wife with a man not their husband (s. 72 (4) and 73 (3) as amended).

If the deceased's death was as a result of pneumoconiosis or a related disease and the conditions of the Pneumoconiosis, etc. (Workers' Compensation) Act 1979 are satisfied, certain "dependants" defined in section 3 of the Act are entitled to claim a lump sum payment. In the absence of a qualified spouse or child, a dependant means "a reputed spouse" who was residing with the deceased. The Act does not define "a reputed spouse."

CONCLUSION

Despite recent developments, the rights of a cohabitee on the death of a partner are far less extensive than the rights of a surviving spouse and the law does not reflect the change in social attitude to unmarried partnerships referred to in *Dyson Holdings Ltd.* v. *Fox*.

Further Reading

Bromley, *Family Law* (Butterworths, 5th ed.).
Cretney, *Principles of Family Law* (Sweet and Maxwell, 3rd ed.).

Eekelaar, *Family Law and Social Policy* (Weidenfeld and Nicolson).

Sweet and Maxwell's Family Law Statutes (2nd ed.).

Arden, *Housing: Security and Rent Control* (Sweet and Maxwell).

Cadwallader, "A Mistresses' Charter?" (1980) Conv. 46.

Calvert, *Social Security Law* (Sweet and Maxwell, 2nd ed.).

Khan, "De Facto 'Family' Under the Rent Act" (1979) 9 Fam. Law 149.

Law Commission, Second Report on Family Property: *Family Provision on Death* (Law Com. No. 61).

Martyn, *The Modern Law of Family Provision* (Sweet and Maxwell).

Poulter, "The Death of a Lover" (1976) 126 N.L.J. 417, 433.

Samuels, "Inheritance (Provision for Family and Dependants) Act 1975" (1976) 39 M.L.R. 183.

Zander, *Social Workers, their Clients and the Law* (Sweet and Maxwell, 3rd ed.).

6 Children

STATUS

1. *Legitimacy and Illegitimacy*

A child's status is dependent upon the status of his parents. The legal relationship between a parent and his child is not based on parenthood alone, but on the concept of legitimacy, which is determined by reference to a valid marriage of the parents. At common law, a child is legitimate if his natural parents are married to each other, either at the time of the child's conception, or at the time of the child's birth. If the parents are not married to each other at either of those times the child is illegitimate.

The law discriminates against the illegitimate child even if he lives in a stable relationship with his parents. Reform of the law has moved some way towards removing the discrimination, for example in questions of inheritance (see *post*, p. 122). The illegitimate child does not, however, enjoy equal treatment with his legitimate brother or sister, and the parents of an illegitimate child do not enjoy equal treatment with the parents of a legitimate child. The reasons are historical. An illegitimate child was *filius nullius*, *i.e.* nobody's child, and no one had rights in respect of him. The law developed in favour of granting rights to the mother (see *Barnado* v. *McHugh* (1891)), but not to the father.

This discrimination may be of little concern to fathers who have shown no interest in their children, but it does affect the father who is living in a stable relationship with the child and the child's mother. The birth registration figures (see *post*, p. 103) suggests that as many as half the illegitimate births are the result of such relationships.

The legal disadvantages of illegitimacy represent only part of the discrimination against the illegitimate child; equally important, and probably more significant, are the social and economic disadvantages. The children of a stable cohabitation will suffer few disadvantages compared with the illegitimate children of one-parent families (see Finer Committee Report on One-Parent Families 1974).

The total number of illegitimate children is significant—about one and a half million recorded births since 1945. The illegitimate birth rate is currently about 10 per cent. of births in England and Wales. Of this number many later acquire the status of legitimacy, either on their parents' marriage, or by adoption. It is increasingly felt, and the Law Commission tentatively favour (see *post*, p. 124) that the status of illegitimacy should be abolished.

2. *Statutory Legitimacy*

The disadvantages attaching to illegitimacy have been lessened by statutory modifications to the common law rule of legitimacy, so that, in certain circumstances, children who would otherwise have been illegitimate are given the status of legitimacy. If the parents' marriage is defective, their children may nevertheless be legitimate. Certain defects, for example, lack of consent to the marriage (see further Matrimonial Causes Act 1973, s. 12) are not regarded as so serious as to render a marriage void. The marriage is voidable, *i.e.* valid until one of the parties has it annulled, and even if the marriage is annulled, any child born or conceived during the marriage is legitimate (Matrimonial Causes Act 1973, s. 16 and Sched. 1, para. 12). Some defects in a marriage, for example if either party is under the age of 16, are so serious that the law demands that there is no marriage at all (see further Matrimonial Causes Act 1973, s. 11). Such marriages are void regardless of any court decree. One would think that as the parents are not married their children would be illegitimate, but they are not necessarily so. The Legitimacy Act 1959 introduced the concept of the "putative marriage" whereby such children are treated as the legitimate children of their parents, if at the time of the child's conception or at the time of marriage if later, either or both of the parents reasonably believed that the marriage was valid (Legitimacy Act 1976, s. 1). The belief need only be held by one of the parents, but it must be resonable. An unreasonable belief, however honestly held, will not do (see *Hawkins* v. *A.-G.* (1966)). For the rule to apply the father must have been domiciled (see *post*, p. 141) in England at the time of the child's birth.

3. *Legitimation*

An illegitimate child acquires the status of legitimacy if his natural parents marry after his birth, provided that the child's father is domiciled in England at the date of marriage (Legitimacy Act 1976, s. 2). The child is legitimated from the date of the marriage. One of the advantages of cohabitees marrying is to legitimate their children. The introduction of divorce on the basis of five years' separation (see *post*, p. 126) enables many spouses, who had been cohabiting with someone else and had illegitimate children, to divorce their spouse in order to marry their cohabitee and legitimate the children. The status of a legitimated child is virtually identical to that of the legitimate child.

After marrying the parents should re-register the birth and they are under a duty to give the necessary information so that re-registration can take place (Legitimacy Act 1976, s. 9; Births and Deaths Registration Act 1953, s. 14).

Legitimation was introduced by the Legitimacy Act 1926 and at first only applied if the child's parents were free to marry at the time of the child's birth. It was felt that to allow legitimation of a child born of adultery would encourage adulterous relationships. It was not until the Legitimacy Act 1959 that adulterine children could be legitimated by their parents' marriage.

An illegitimate child is also legitimated if he is adopted. He is then treated as the legitimate child of the adopter(s) (Children Act 1975, Sched. 1, paras. 3 and 4; Adoption Act 1976, ss. 39 and 41). The adoptive parent may be one of the natural parents (see Legitimacy Act 1976, s. 4), but such adoptions are rare (Children Act 1975, s. 11 (3); Adoption Act 1976, s. 15 (3), see *post*, p. 110).

4. *Presumption of Legitimacy*

The common law rule of legitimacy has also been modified by the "presumption of legitimacy," i.e. that a child born to a married woman is presumed to be her husband's child. If the wife is separated from her husband and cohabiting with another man, does the presumption operate so that the child is presumed to be the legitimate child of the husband? If the husband and wife are separated by a court order entitling them to live apart (for example, a judicial separation or a magistrates' court order incorporating a non-cohabitation clause) at the time of conception, the presumption does not operate. If they are separated by agreement the presumption will, however, apply.

The presumption can be rebutted. At one time the presumption could only be rebutted by evidence beyond reasonable doubt, but now it is up to the person alleging that the child is illegitimate to prove that the presumption is rebutted on a balance of probabilities (Family Law Reform Act 1969, s. 26). This can be shown, for example, by proving that the husband was incapable of having intercourse at the time, either because he was impotent or because he did not have access to his wife. It could also be shown by proving that, notwithstanding that the husband could have had intercourse, he is not the father, for example, if the husband was sterile or by blood test evidence (see *post*, p. 118), or by dissimilarities in colour, for example, if the child is half-caste and the mother and her husband are both white. The presumption is now easily rebutted for: "... even weak evidence against legitimacy must prevail if there is not other evidence to counterbalance it." (Lord Reid in *S* v. *S* (1970).)

BIRTH REGISTRATION

The law requires the registration of all births in England and Wales (Births and Deaths Registration Act 1953, ss. 1 and 2 as amended by Children Act 1975). Before the Children Act 1975 the only circumstances in which the birth of an illegitimate child could be registered or re-registered to show the father's name were either at his and the mother's joint request, or at the mother's request on production of a declaration by her that the man was the father, together with a statutory declaration by him acknowledging paternity. Registration of the father's name was not possible if he disputed paternity. The 1975 Act now permits this at the mother's written request, where the man has been named as the putative father in an affiliation order and, if the child has attained the age of 16, the child gives his written consent (1953 Act, s. 10 as amended by Family Law Reform Act 1969, s. 27 and 1975 Act, s. 93).

The decision to register the father's name always rests in part with the mother. Without the mother's consent the father cannot have his name registered even if he is cohabiting with the mother, or he has been named as father in an affiliation order, or if there is a custody or access order in his favour. The mother can register the father's name without his consent if there is an affiliation order naming him. Approximately half the illegitimate births are registered on the joint application of both parents.

If the birth was originally registered without the father's name the birth can be re-registered so as to include it, provided that one of the three conditions above, which would enable registration under section 10 of the 1953 Act, is satisfied (1953 Act, s. 10A as inserted by 1975 Act, s. 93 (2)).

Registration of a man as the child's father does not affect the legal relationship between him and the child and confers no rights upon the man, but will be evidence of paternity (1953 Act, s. 34; *Jackson* v. *Jackson* (1960)) and can be relied upon, for example, in affiliation proceedings, or to claim succession rights.

A birth certificate is a certified copy of the entry in the register of births, and is evidence of the birth to which it relates (1953 Act, s. 34 (6)). A "long form" of certificate discloses parentage but a "short form" of certificate makes no reference to the child's parents (1953 Act,

s. 33). The intention of the short form is that it will not reveal that the father's name is not registered, or that the father is not married to the mother and that the child is thus illegitimate. The form merely gives the name, surname, sex, date and place of birth of the child (Birth Certificate (Shortened Form) Regulations 1968). A short form will be issued free on registration of the birth and will usually be issued on application for a birth certificate unless the long form is requested. Nevertheless, the majority of certificates issued are in the long form, and the infrequent use of the short form in respect of legitimate children has meant that it is not as successful as intended in concealing the illegitimate child's status.

So far as the surname registered for the illegitimate child, the choice is one of the parental rights vested solely in the mother (see below). Where the parents are cohabiting, the mother may prefer to register the surname of the man, rather than her own, particularly if she holds herself out as his wife. Surnames may be changed at will. The right to change the illegitimate child's surname is also vested in the mother and in due course the child himself.

PARENTAL RIGHTS AND DUTIES

1. *What are Parental Rights and Duties?*

It is not possible within this book to do more than list some of the parental rights and duties (for further details see Hoggett, *Parents and Children*, Chapter 1). They have been said to include rights to custody, access, determine the child's upbringing (including education and religion), discipline, choose medical treatment, choose surname, allow the child to go abroad, consent to marriage under 18, appoint a guardian, agree to adoption, administer the child's property and corresponding duties to protect, maintain, educate and provide necessary medical treatment. All parental rights and duties are usually part of custody in its wide meaning. Their exercise and enforcement diminishes as the child grows older so that this "bundle of rights" is better seen as a "bundle of powers" (*Hewer* v. *Bryant* (1969)).

2. *Who has Parental Rights and Duties?*

Generally, "while the mother of an illegitimate child is living she has the parental rights and duties exclusively" (Children Act 1975, s. 85 (7)). This is in marked contrast to parental rights and duties in respect of legitimate children, which are enjoyed by both parents equally (Guardianship Act 1973, s. 1 (1)). The male partner of a stable cohabitation prima facie has no rights over the children of the union, regardless of the length and stability of the relationship. He does have the right to apply to the court for custody (see below). He may also have obligations towards the child, for example, if, as will be the case in many cohabitations, the child is living with both parents, the father will be under a duty to educate the child and ensure that the child is not neglected or ill-treated, for these responsibilities fall on anyone who has care of a child (see for example, Children and Young Persons Act 1933, s. 1).

During a stable cohabitation the exercise of parental rights and duties is unlikely to be in issue. Their exercise will be of importance, however, on breakdown of cohabitation when the advice of a social worker may be sought. In particular the mother may wish to seek maintenance for the child, from the father (see *post*, p. 114), and there may be a dispute as to custody of the child.

3. Custody

Custody in its wide sense means all parental rights and duties. The term is also used in a narrow sense to mean possession of the child, sometimes referred to as "care and control" of the child. The complexity of terminology does nothing to help the understanding of the law, for:

"... somewhat confusingly one of the powers conferred by custody in its wide meaning is custody in its limited meaning." (Sachs L.J. in *Hewer* v. *Bryant* (1969).)

The father of an illegitimate child has no rights of guardianship, custody or access, but statute has given him the right to apply to a magistrates' court, county court or the High Court for custody, or as it is now called, legal custody (Guardianship of Minors Act 1971, ss. 9 (1) and 14 (1) as amended by Domestic Proceedings and Magistrates' Courts Act 1978, s. 36). Legal custody means "so much of the parental rights and duties as relate to the person of the child (including the place and manner in which his time is spent)" (1978 Act, s. 36; Children Act 1975, s. 86). For the sake of simplicity the term custody will be used in the following discussion.

The father of an illegitimate child who is cohabiting with the child's mother, is only likely to apply for custody in the event of a dispute with the mother. In deciding any such application, the child's welfare is the first and paramount consideration (Guardianship of Minors Act 1971,

s. 1). In reality it is often difficult for the father of a legitimate child to obtain custody and it has proved even more difficult for the father of an illegitimate child to do so, on the basis that such a father has no parental rights.

The courts are now tending to the view, however, that it is in a child's interests to maintain contact with both his parents and it matters not that the child is illegitimate (see, for example, *S.* v. *O.* (1978) and contrast *Re G.* (1956)). The longer and more stable the relationship between father and child, the greater the father's chances of obtaining custody (see, for example, *Re H.* (1965)), or if not custody, at least access to the child. Where a child has enjoyed such a relationship, it may well be in his interests to continue it (see, generally, *M.* v. *M.* (1973)). It has been said that:

"... a court should be extremely slow to shut out either parent when the parents and child have lived together under the same roof." (Sir George Baker in *M.* v. *J.* (1977).)

There is no power under the Guardianship of Minors Act 1971 to make orders regarding maintenance for the child (s. 14 (2)). In so far as the mother can claim such maintenance, she has to rely on the less satisfactory affiliation proceedings, which by their nature discourage applicants (see *post*, p. 116).

The law further discriminates against the father of an illegitimate child, in comparison with the mother for, unlike the father of a legitimate child, even if he is granted custody, he cannot obtain maintenance for the child from the mother. He will, however, on being granted custody, acquire certain additional rights. Some he will have jointly with the child's mother, for example the right to appoint a testamentary guardian (Guardianship of Minors Act 1971, ss. 4 and 14 (3)), others he will have to the exclusion of the mother, for example the right to agree to the child's marriage below the age of 18 (Marriage Act 1949, Sched. II).

A custody order in favour of the father of an illegitimate child makes him a "guardian" for purposes of the child's adoption (Children Act 1975, s. 107 (1); Adoption Act 1976, s. 72 (1)) and as such, his agreement to the child's adoption is required, together with that of the mother, who alone is regarded as a "parent" (see *post*, p. 111).

A custody order under the 1971 Act remains in force if the parents continue to cohabit or resume cohabitation, but ceases to be enforceable if they live together for more than 6 months (Domestic Proceedings and Magistrates' Courts Act 1978, s. 46).

The illegitimate child's father was given the right to apply for custody or access by the Legitimacy Act 1959. His remedy before that date, which is now available as an alternative, was to apply to have the child made a ward of court and for him to be awarded "care and control," custody being vested in the court. This procedure, which is available to anyone with an interest in the child's upbringing, is not to be recommended in view of the father's right to apply for custody, because it is expensive and impractical. Proceedings have to be brought in the High Court and the exercise of parental rights and duties, other than care and control, rests with the court. If an illegitimate child is made a ward of court, the court has no power, as it does in the case of a legitimate child, to order either parent to pay maintenance for the child (Family Law Reform Act 1969, s. 6 (6)).

4. *Joint Parental Rights and Duties*

Can unmarried parents who are cohabiting share parental rights and duties? In practice, many do, but any agreement to give up parental rights over a legitimate child is unenforceable unless it is to operate during the parents' separation, in which case the agreement is enforceable unless the court thinks it is not for the child's benefit (Guardianship Act 1973, s. 1 (2)). That provision does not apply to an illegitimate child (s. 1 (7)), but the Children Act 1975 provides that: "Subject to section 1 (2) of the Guardianship Act 1973 ... a person cannot surrender or transfer to another any parental right or duty he has as respects a child" (s. 85 (2)). The subsection enacts the previous common law rule and, it is submitted, applies to the illegitimate child, so the mother of an illegitimate child cannot enter into an agreement with the father to share parental rights and duties. The parents of a legitimate child can do so only in the exceptional circumstances set out in s. 1 (2) of the Guardianship Act 1973. The Law Commission have suggested the repeal of s. 1 (2), so that there would be no power to enter into an enforceable agreement about parental rights in respect of any children (Law Com. No. 74, paras. 4.21 to 4.25).

It is theoretically possible for parents who are not married but who are cohabiting, to apply for a joint custody order under section 9 of the Guardianship of Minors Act 1971, but such orders cease to be enforceable if the parents live together for more than 6 months (Domestic Proceedings and Magistrates' Courts Act 1978, s. 46). Such parents cannot acquire joint parental rights by adoption nor by custodianship (see *post*, p. 110 and p. 112). Guardianship is only available on the mother's death (see below). If they marry they will, of course, thereafter have joint parental rights and duties.

If there are children of a cohabitation of whom only one of the partners is the parent, the non-parent will neither enjoy parental rights nor have much chance to acquire any. Applications for custody under the Guardianship of Minors Act 1971 are limited to parents (s. 9). A non-parent can apply to the High Court for the child to be made a ward of court and seek care and control or access, but such proceedings are expensive and impractical. When the custodianship provisions of the Children Act 1975 come into force, the non-parent could seek a custodianship order, but the parties would not have joint custody, for any custodianship order would suspend the custody of the parent (see *post*, p. 113). If such a child has been the subject of a custody order in divorce proceedings, the order could, in theory, be varied in favour of the parent and his or her cohabitee (Matrimonial Causes Act 1973, s. 42).

5. *Parental Rights and Duties on the Mother's Death*

Where the parents of an illegitimate child are cohabiting, the child's father acquires no right to custody of the child on the mother's death. On the death of a parent of a legitimate child, the surviving parent will normally have sole custody as sole guardian (Guardianship of Minors Act 1971, s. 3, see further Hoggett, *op. cit.*, Chap. 7). The rule does not apply in the case of an illegitimate child, because parental rights and duties are vested solely in the mother. The father is not a guardian by virtue of parenthood.

On termination of cohabitation by the mother's death, the father does not become guardian, unless the mother appointed him guardian in her will or in a deed to take effect on her death (Guardianship of Minors Act 1971, s. 4), or unless he obtains a court order appointing him guardian, or has already been awarded custody by a court (Guardianship of Minors Act 1971, ss. 3 (2) and 14 (3)).

In many cases when the mother of an illegitimate child dies, the child is without a guardian, so the court can, if it thinks fit, on the application of anyone, appoint the applicant to be the child's guardian (Guardianship of Minors Act 1971, s. 5). Otherwise, as there is no guardian, it is the duty of the local authority to receive the child into care (see below).

The father of an illegitimate child who had been cohabiting in a stable relationship with the child's mother and the child, would be advised, on the mother's death, to invoke section 5 of the Guardianship of Minors Act 1971, rather than rely on *de facto* care of the child. To avoid his having to do so, however, the mother should appoint the father testamentary guardian of the child in her will, which would prevent the child being received into care on the ground that he has no guardian. The father has no power to appoint a testamentary guardian unless he has been awarded custody by a court order which is still in force on his death (Guardianship of Minors Act 1971, s. 14 (3)).

6. *Children in Care*

The fact that the unmarried mother has sole parental rights and duties is important if the child is in care of the local authority, for, generally, the mother alone is a "parent" for the purposes of the Children Act 1948 (see s. 59 (1)) (Child Care Act 1980, see s. 87 (1) and the Children and Young Persons Act 1969).

Section 1 of the 1948 Act (1980 Act, s. 2) provides for the reception into care of children whose parents are not able to look after them. The essence of the section is the voluntary placing of the child in care: the local authority does not have the right to keep the child if a parent or guardian wishes to take over the care of the child (1948 Act, s. 1 (3); 1980 Act, s. 2 (3)). Suppose, for example, the mother and father are cohabiting, the mother is taken into hospital and so the local authority agrees to receive the children into care under the 1948 Act, section 1 (1980 Act, s. 2). The children's father later decides he can cope with looking after them, notwithstanding their mother's absence, and requests their return. Under the 1948 Act he is not a "parent" and so not entitled to take over the care of the children himself, although as a "relative" he could be allowed to take over their care if it appeared to the authority to be consistent with the children's welfare. The 1980 Act, as a consolidating Act, has not changed the position (see s. 87 (1)). Should the father successfully apply for custody of the children, he then stands in the place of the mother (1948 Act, s. 6 (2); 1980 Act, s. 8 (2)) and thus entitled to the care of the children, unless the local authority passes a 1948 Act, section 2 resolution (1980 Act, section 3 resolution) or institutes wardship proceedings. The problem remains, of course, that if the mother and father enjoy a stable relationship, he is unlikely to want to jeopardise it by taking custody proceedings.

Where a section 2 resolution (1980 Act, section 3 resolution) is passed in respect of an illegitimate child, the resolution vests the mother's parental rights and duties in the local authority, but not those of the father. In particular, his right to apply for custody under the Guardianship of Minors Act 1971, s. 9 is unaffected (*R.* v. *Oxford City Justices, ex p. H.* (1974)). The matter should be left to the court to decide in the light of all the circumstances, including the resolution, on the basis that the child's welfare is the first and paramount consideration. Where the issue is one of access to the child, rather than care, the court may well decide that the matter is best left to the local authority's discretion as part of their day to day control (*Re K.* (1972)).

The Children and Young Persons Act 1969 provides for the taking of proceedings for the care of children who are in need of care or control, which they will not receive unless the court makes an order. In addition, one of seven conditions must be satisfied, one of which is that the child is beyond the control of his parent or guardian. The term "parent" is not defined, so the normal rule applies and it will not include the father of an illegitimate child. The meaning of the term "guardian" in the Children and Young Persons Acts (1933 Act, s. 107 (1); 1969 Act, s. 70 (1)) is sufficiently wide, however, to include a cohabiting father. The term includes anyone who, for the time being, has the charge of, or control over, the child or young person.

ADOPTION

1. *What is Adoption?*

Adoption is the transference of all parental rights and duties from the natural parents to the adopters (Children Act 1975, s. 8; Adoption Act 1976, s. 12). An adoption order involves a change of status, the natural parents cease to be parents and the child becomes the child of the adoptive parents. He is regarded as their legitimate child (1975 Act, Sched. 1, para. 3; 1976 Act, s. 39: on adoption generally see Hoggett, *op. cit.*, Chapter 11).

Adoption may concern cohabitees either as adopters, or as parents whose child is being adopted.

2. *Who can Adopt?*

A joint adoption application can only be made by a married couple (1975 Act, s. 10 (1); 1976 Act, s. 14 (1)), so cohabitees cannot jointly adopt their own child, the child of one of them, or any other child. In one case an adoption order was granted to joint adopters whose marriage was void. The court decided that the adoption was valid unless and until set aside by the court (*Re F.* (1977)).

An adoption application can be made by one person, provided he is over 21 and not married, or is married but his spouse cannot be found, is incapable of making an adoption application because of ill health, or they are living apart and the separation is likely to be permanent (1975 Act, s. 11 (1); 1976 Act, s. 15 (1)). A cohabitee who satisfies these requirements is thus theoretically qualified to apply as a sole adopter. A court will, however, be reluctant to make such an order, particularly if the sole applicant is a parent. An adoption order cannot be made in favour of one natural parent unless the other natural parent is dead or cannot be found, or there is some other reason justifying the exclusion of the other natural parent (1975 Act, s. 11 (3); 1976 Act, s. 15 (3)). It is submitted that this restriction applies to the illegitimate child as well as the legitimate (see Bevan and Parry, *Children Act 1975*, para. 96) and that the term "natural parent" includes the father of an illegitimate child, notwithstanding that he is not a "parent" for adoption law, but a "relative" (see Bevan and Parry, *op. cit.*, para. 97).

The restriction does not apply if the other parent is dead. The mother is unlikely to apply if the father is dead as she will already have parental rights and duties, but the provision could help the father on the mother's death if he wishes to establish a legal relationship with the child. Alternatively he could apply to be appointed the child's guardian (Guardianship of Minors Act 1971, s. 5, see above).

3. *Agreement to Adoption*

A child cannot be adopted unless the court is satisfied that each parent or guardian of the child agrees to the adoption, or that his agreement can be dispensed with on one of the specified grounds (1975 Act, s. 12; 1976 Act, s. 16). The father of an illegitimate child is not, however, a "parent" (*Re M.* (1955)), and thus only the mother's agreement is required, unless the father has custody by virtue of an order under section 9 of the Guardianship of Minors Act 1971 (see *ante*, p. 105), or the mother is dead and she appointed him guardian in her will.

Where cohabitees enjoy a stable relationship, they will, no doubt, decide jointly about their child's adoption. Where the parties have split up, however, and the father is liable to maintain a child under an affiliation order or by agreement, he must be notified of the hearing of the adoption application, so that his views can be heard (Adoption (High Court) Rules 1976, r. 18; Adoption (County Court) Rules 1976, r. 4; Magistrates' Courts (Adoption) Rules 1976, r. 4). If the father is not so liable, the court is under no duty to seek him out, but if anyone is claiming to be the father and wishes to be heard, the court should be informed (see Sched. 2, para. 10 of the Rules). The father's agreement to the adoption is not, however, required.

The father could frustrate the adoption application by applying for custody or by making the child a ward of court. If he does so apply, the custody or wardship application and the adoption application should be heard together and decided on the basis that the child's welfare is the first and paramount consideration (see *Re Adoption Application No. 41/61* (1962) and *Re C. (M.A.)* (1966)).

Where the father has enjoyed a stable relationship with the mother and the child, the ties between him and the child are likely to be as strong as those between father and legitimate child. In past years the courts have not attached much weight to the wishes of the father of an illegitimate child, on the basis that the advantages of adoption and the removal of the status of illegitimacy outweigh the disadvantages associated with the severance of links with the natural father (see, for example, *Re E. (P.)* (1969)). More recently the courts have reflected the change in attitude towards illegitimacy and given increased recognition to the tie between illegitimate child and father, so that, in exceptional cases, the court has regarded access by the father as in the child's best interests and made an adoption order conditional on access by the father (*Re J.* (1973); *Re S.* (1975)). In future when it is felt desirable that the father should not lose all contact with his child, custodianship will be an alternative to adoption.

CUSTODIANSHIP

1. *What is Custodianship?*

Custodianship is a new concept which was introduced by the Children Act 1975. When the custodianship provisions come into force they will enable certain qualified persons, other than the child's mother or father, to apply to the court for "legal custody" of the child. If the court makes a custodianship order it will grant legal custody to the applicant who becomes the child's "custodian" (1975 Act, s. 33 (1) and (2)). Custodianship is for non-parents and is intended primarily for relatives, step-parents and long-term foster parents, as an alternative to adoption or wardship. A custodian has "legal custody" in the same way as has a parent who is granted legal custody under section 9 of the Guardianship of Minors Act 1971, *i.e.* "so much of the parental rights and duties as relate to the person of the child (including the place and manner in which his time is spent); but a person shall not by virtue of having legal custody of a child be entitled to effect or arrange for his emigration from the United Kingdom unless he is a parent or guardian of the child" (1975 Act, s. 86).

Custodianship has the advantage over adoption that it does not sever all links with the natural parents, and the order can be revoked.

2. *Who can Apply?*

The child's mother or father cannot apply for a custodianship order (1975 Act, s. 33 (4)). They do not need to, for their remedy is to apply for legal custody under section 9 of the Guardianship of Minors Act 1971 and only parents can apply under that jurisdiction (see *ante*,

p. 105). Cohabitees cannot, therefore, apply for a custodianship order in respect of their own child as a means of acquiring joint parental rights and duties. The parental exclusion must extend to the father of an illegitimate child, for he too has the right to apply for legal custody under section 9 of the 1971 Act. He may not be a "parent" for adoption purposes, but surely he must be a "father" for custodianship purposes. It would be illogical if the exclusion in section 33 (4) did not apply to the putative father for he, and only he, would then be qualified to apply under either section 9 of the 1971 Act or section 33 of the 1975 Act.

An application is not barred by a non-parent. If a couple are cohabiting as man and wife together with a child of whom only one is a parent, the non-parent could, if he otherwise qualifies, apply for a custodianship order, but the effect of such an order would be to suspend the parent's rights to legal custody (1975 Act, s. 44 (1)). For example, the mother of an illegitimate child cohabits with a man who is not the child's father. The man applies for and is granted a custodianship order. The mother's rights to legal custody are suspended. That result does not occur if the mother marries, rather than cohabits with, a man who is not the child's father, for if the applicant for a custodianship order is a spouse of the parent and an order is made, the spouses have joint legal custody of the child (s. 44 (2)).

In deciding the application, the child's welfare, as in all custody applications, is the first and paramount consideration (1975 Act, s. 33 (9)). If a non-parent applicant and a parent are living together, the court is going to take a lot of convincing that the suspension of the parent's rights is in the child's interests. In the event of a breakdown of the cohabitation, the chances of a non-parent being awarded legal custody cannot be any higher than the chances of the father of an illegitimate child succeeding in a custody application (see *ante*, p. 106).

A joint application for a custodianship order is not possible if either of the applicants is the child's mother or father (see above), but a joint application by two non parents is not so barred, even if the applicants are unmarried. So an unmarried couple living together as man and wife could apply for legal custody of someone else's child if they are otherwise qualified (see below), whereas they could not apply to adopt the child. A custodianship order could likewise be of help in the case of a family cohabitation, for example an order could be made on the application of a brother and sister caring for a child, even though they could not make a joint adoption application. The nature and stability of the applicants' relationship will be one of the matters to be taken into account by the court when considering the application.

To qualify to apply for a custodianship order, the applicant, or applicants, must satisfy section 33 (3) of the Children Act 1975. Cohabitees should apply jointly so that legal custody can be vested in them both. There are three circumstances in which the applicants will be qualified to apply.

First, if they are relatives of the child who has had his home with them for the three months before the application and a person with legal custody consents to the application. The same applies to applications by step-parents, but only a spouse of a parent is a step-parent and thus the special provisions relating to applications by step-parents do not apply to cohabitees (see ss. 33 (3) (*a*), (5), (8); 37 (1), (5), Bevan and Parry, *op. cit.*, paras. 259–261, 276–277).

Second, if they are not relatives, the child must have had his home with them for at least 12 months (not necessarily in one period) including the three months before the application and provided they have the same consent. Usually the parents will have legal custody, in which case only one of them need consent. If the child is the subject of a resolution under section 2 of the Children Act 1948 (s. 3 of the Child Care Act 1980), or of a care order under the Children and Young Persons Act 1969 (see *ante*, p. 109) then the local authority and not a parent must consent.

Third, in the absence of the consent of a person with legal custody, the child must have had his home with the applicants for a period or periods of at least three years before the application, including the previous three months. If consent is not forthcoming, it cannot be dispensed with.

If the child of cohabitees is the subject of a custodianship application, the mother will usually be the only person able to consent to the application, because the father of an illegitimate child will not be a person having legal custody, unless he has been awarded it under section 9 of the Guardianship of Minors Act 1971.

The father of an illegitimate child cannot be required to pay maintenance for the child to the person who has been awarded legal custody under a custodianship order (1975 Act, s. 34 (3)). This provision is in line with the general law relating to the father's liability to maintain his illegitimate child which is based on affiliation proceedings (see below).

MAINTENANCE

1. *Maintenance by Parent*

One of the parental duties is the duty to maintain. Where unmarried parents live together, with children, in a stable relationship, the question of enforcing the duty is unlikely to arise, but should the parents fail to maintain the children, the advice of social workers may be sought regarding maintenance. The duty can be enforced in one of three ways.

Supplementary benefits

For supplementary benefits purposes, both parents are liable to maintain their children under the age of 16 (Supplementary Benefits Act 1976, ss. 17 and 34, as amended by Social Security Act 1980). The rule applies to both legitimate and illegitimate children, provided that in the case of the latter, the man has been adjudged to be the putative father (1976 Act, s. 17 (2)). If a parent fails to maintain his child and as a result supplementary benefit is provided for the child, the Secretary of State can seek to recover the money paid, by taking proceedings in a magistrates' court against "the liable person" (1976 Act, s. 18, as amended by 1980 Act).

To recover benefit from the father of an illegitimate child, the Secretary of State must apply under section 19 of the 1976 Act (and see *Robinson* v. *Lowther* (1980)) and rely either on an existing affiliation order in the mother's favour by having it varied in favour of the Secretary of State (1976 Act, s. 19 (4), (5), as amended by 1980 Act) or, in the absence of an affiliation order, by applying for one (1976 Act, s. 19 (2), as amended by Domestic Proceedings and Magistrates' Courts Act 1978, Sched. 2, para. 54). The Secretary of State can apply for an affiliation order within three years of paying any benefit and can do so, notwithstanding a previous unsuccessful application by the mother (*Clapham* v. *National Assistance Board* (1961)). Few such applications are in fact made. More usual is "the diversion procedure" under which payments under an affiliation order in favour of the mother are paid to the supplementary benefit authorities. The mother authorises the court to pay over any maintenance received and in return she is paid her full benefit, regardless of whether or not the father pays the order.

The mother's concern will, of course, be with getting more money from somewhere. Her right to supplementary benefit does not depend on her, or the Secretary of State, obtaining an affiliation order against the father. The official policy is to discuss with the woman her taking affiliation proceedings, but the decision whether or not to take her own proceedings is left to her. Whatever she decides, she will continue to receive the full benefit to which she is entitled. In many cases she will have nothing to gain by taking affiliation proceedings, for the amount received will often be less than her supplementary benefit entitlement. It is questionable whether or not in practice sufficient regard is paid, when advising mothers, to the financial inadequacies of affiliation orders.

Affiliation proceedings

The nature of affiliation proceedings, which are based on the old Poor Law, and the embarrassment caused to the mother, discourage applicants. It is not surprising, therefore, that only a small proportion of mothers of illegitimate children take such proceedings, particularly if there is the prospect of the parents starting or continuing a stable relationship. Many illegitimate children live in such a relationship and, in view of the increasing number of cohabitations, the whole basis of the parental duty to maintain is open to question, for although proceedings are unlikely during the continuance of cohabitation, this is not so on breakdown of such a relationship, when the mother's need will be particularly acute, because she cannot seek maintenance from her partner for herself (see *ante*, p. 36). She is therefore at a disadvantage in comparison to a wife on breakdown of marriage. Moreover insufficient attention is given to provision for the child. The rules which follow seem hard to justify.

(i) *Who can apply?* To seek maintenance for the child from the child's father, the mother must apply to a magistrates' court for an affiliation order under the Affiliation Proceedings Act 1957 (1957 Act), as amended by the Affiliation Proceedings (Amendment) Act 1972 and the Domestic Proceedings and Magistrates' Courts Act 1978. To apply, the mother must be a "single woman" at the time of the application or at the time of the child's birth (1957 Act, s. 1; Legitimacy Act 1959, s. 4). An unmarried mother is a single woman, as is a widow and a divorced woman, but the phrase is not limited to the unmarried, for a married woman who is separated from her husband and who has lost the common law right to be maintained by him, is included. Thus, a wife who had committed adultery has been held to be a single woman (*Jones* v. *Evans* (1945)). It may be, however, that such a wife is no longer a single woman as she can now apply for maintenance under her statutory right to be maintained, notwithstanding her adultery (Domestic Proceedings and Magistrates' Courts Act 1978).

An application can be made before the child's birth but will not be heard until after the birth. Applications must normally be made within three years of the birth (1957 Act, s. 2 (1) (*a*), as amended by the Affiliation Proceedings (Amendment) Act 1972, s. 2 (1)). This rule would be unjust in cases where the mother had not applied for an order within the time limit because the father had been maintaining the child, for example because the child's parents were cohabiting. Thus the time limit does not apply if the man has maintained the child within the first three years of its life (1957 Act, s. 2 (1) (*b*), as amended by 1972 Act, s. 2 (1)). Where an unmarried couple have cohabited as man and wife and an illegitimate child was a member of the family, it will be presumed, until the contrary is shown, that the man has maintained the child (see *Roberts* v. *Roberts* (1962)). If the man left the country within the same three year period, the mother may apply within 12 months of his return (1957 Act, s. 2 (1) (*c*), as amended by 1972 Act, s. 2 (1)). If the mother does not apply within the time limit, an application by the Secretary of State may still be possible (see above and *N.A.B.* v. *Mitchell* (1955)). Similarly, if an illegitimate child is in care, the local authority can apply, within three years of the child going into care, for an affiliation order if the mother has not done so (Children Act 1948, s. 26; Child Care Act 1980, s. 50). In either case, application can be made even if the mother is not a single woman (see, for example, *N.A.B.* v. *Tugby* (1957)). There is also provision for the custodian of an illegitimate child, who is not married to the child's mother, to apply for an affiliation order within three years of the making of a custodianship order (Children Act 1975, s. 45 and see *ante*, p. 114). It does not matter that the mother is not a single woman. It also seems that an affiliation order may be made on the application of the person who has the custody of the child either legally or by any arrangement approved by the court (1957 Act, s. 5 (3), as amended by Domestic Proceedings and Magistrates' Courts Act 1978, s. 51 (2)).

The child himself cannot apply for an affiliation order, although if he is over 16, he can apply for the variation of an existing order (1957 Act, s. 6A as inserted by Domestic Proceedings and Magistrates' Courts Act 1978, s. 53).

(ii) *The application.* If the mother is qualified to apply and is within the time limit, she may issue a summons against the alleged father. The police often serve the summons, notwithstanding that the proceedings are civil and not criminal. Indeed, the procedure is more akin to criminal proceedings (for example, appeal to the Crown Court). Affiliation proceedings are heard before the magistrates' court, usually for the area where the mother lives (1957 Act, s. 3, as amended by Domestic Proceedings and Magistrates' Courts Act 1978, s. 49). The proceedings are "domestic proceedings" and are thus in private with restricted press reporting (Affiliation Proceedings (Amendment) Act 1972, s. 3).

(iii) *Proof.* The mother must prove her allegation that the man is the father. Paternity is, for obvious reasons, more difficult to prove than maternity. The mother is not bound to give evidence, but as she has to prove her case she will usually do so unless there is an admission of paternity. If she does give evidence it must be corroborated in some material particular by other evidence (1957 Act, s. 4 (1), as amended by Affiliation Proceedings (Amendment) Act 1972, s. 1).

In many cases paternity is admitted. One study indicated that paternity was disputed in only a quarter of applications (see further, Report of Committee on Statutory Maintenance Limits 1968, para. 185). The man can admit paternity by, for example, having allowed himself to be registered as the child's father (see *ante*, p. 103). Where the mother and father have cohabited in a stable relationship, the mother will seek to rely on the father's maintenance of the child as an admission of paternity.

If paternity is disputed, the mother may wish to rely on blood test evidence. A blood test cannot directly establish who is the father of a child, but it can conclusively establish who is not the father. The chance of excluding a non-father using the different blood group systems is at least 70 per cent. and possibly as high as 90 per cent. If the test does not exclude the alleged father, the particular blood group characteristics are determined and the frequency of these occurring is expressed as a percentage of the general population. If such men are not very frequent and the alleged father, not having been excluded, is one of them, the court is likely to decide that, on the balance of probabilities, he is the father. Similarly, if there is evidence that only two men had intercourse with the mother and the blood test evidence excludes one of them, then by elimination the other must be the father.

The courts' powers with regard to blood tests are contained in the Family Law Reform Act 1969, Part III, which confers a discretion on the court, in any civil proceedings in which the paternity of any person is in issue, to direct blood tests to be taken from that person, the mother and anyone alleged to be the father (s. 20 (1)). The court cannot order a person to be blood tested, it can only direct, so anyone over 16 can refuse (s. 21 (1) (2)). In the case of a child under 16, the consent of the person with care and control is required (s. 21 (3)). If a person refuses to be tested, the court is entitled to draw such inferences from the refusal as appear proper (s. 23), for example, that person may not be able to rely on the presumption of legitimacy (see *ante*, p. 102).

Blood test evidence has become increasingly significant in affiliation proceedings and the court usually exercises its discretion in favour of directing tests because the outcome will not affect the child's status. In view of the reliability of blood test evidence, the time limits on applying for an affiliation order appear questionable.

(iv) *The order.* If the mother is successful, then the man is adjudged the "putative father" and an affiliation order may be made against him. The types of order available have been enlarged by the Domestic Proceedings and Magistrates' Courts Act 1978, ss. 49–53, on the recommendation of the Law Commission.

An order can be made for periodical payments for the child's maintenance and education (1957 Act, s. 4 (2), as substituted by 1978 Act, s. 50 (1)). No limit is set upon the amount of maintenance, but most orders are for small amounts because of the low income of the father. A cohabitee who takes affiliation proceedings against her former partner, who has a good income, is entitled to expect more than the average amount awarded. Such awards should not be limited to subsistence level (*Haroutunian* v. *Jennings* (1977)). There is no reason why the father of an illegitimate child should pay less maintenance for the child on breakdown of cohabitation than the father of a legitimate child has to pay for his child's maintenance on breakdown of marriage.

The court can order a lump sum payment of up to £500, as well as, or instead of, periodical payments (1957 Act, s. 4 (2) (*b*) and (5), as substituted by 1978 Act, s. 50 (1) (2)). The lump sum can be for expenses incurred before the order was made, provided they were incurred in connection with the birth (for example, providing a layette, *Foy* v. *Brooks* (1977)), or in maintaining the child or, if the child has died, funeral expenses.

The child himself cannot apply for an order, but payment may be ordered in favour of the mother on the child's behalf, or to the child himself (1957 Act, s. 5 (1), as amended by 1978 Act, s. 51 (1)). There is, of course, no power to award maintenance for the mother herself. No order can be made if the child has reached the age of 18. Payments can continue until the child's birthday after school leaving age unless the court specifies a later date, but not normally beyond the age of 18. The order ceases on the death of the father or of the child (1957 Act, s. 6, as substituted by 1978 Act, s. 52).

An order may be later varied both as to the amount payable (1957 Act, s. 6A, as inserted by 1978 Act, s. 53) and the person to whom it is paid (1957 Act, s. 5 (3), as amended by 1978 Act, s. 51 (2)).

An affiliation order imposes upon the father the duty to maintain his child, it does not confer upon him corresponding parental rights. He does not become entitled to custody or access and acquires no rights of guardianship. He does not become a parent for adoption purposes, but he does acquire the right to be informed of any adoption proceedings (see *ante*, p. 111). To acquire parental rights, the father must apply for custody in separate proceedings under the Guardianship of Minors Act 1971 (see *ante*, p. 105).

Maintenance agreement

It is to the advantage of all concerned if the father agrees to maintain the child. Such an agreement is enforceable (*Ward* v. *Byham* (1956)) except in so far as it attempts to exclude the mother from applying to the courts for maintenance (*Follit* v. *Koetzow* (1860)). Cohabitees should seek legal advice on the drawing up of an agreement. The court has no power to vary such agreements and the Law Commission have suggested that such a power should be available (Working Paper No. 74, paras. 4.59–4.63).

The law's encouragement of unmarried parents to provide by agreement for the maintenance of their children is to be welcomed. It is noticeable, however, that the law has yet to recognise directly enforceable agreements to maintain made between cohabitees themselves (see Chapter 3). Support obligations, even to the extent of providing a home, have been enforced indirectly, by the use of the concepts of the trust and the licence, particularly where there are children (see *Eves* v. *Eves* (1975), *ante*, p. 17 and *Tanner* v. *Tanner* (1975), *ante*, p. 26). Once again, however, there is little coherence or consistency in the legal approach and the development of the law has been one of accident rather than design.

2. *Maintenance by Non-parent*

The liability to maintain a child normally rests with the child's parents. If either of the parents of an illegitimate child is married to a third party, it is possible for the child to be a "child of the family" of the third party for the purposes of matrimonial law and for the third party to be liable to maintain the child. The matrimonial legislation provides that a "child of the family" includes a child which is not a child of both of the spouses but who has been treated by them as a child of their family (Matrimonial Causes Act 1973, s. 52 (1); Domestic Proceedings and Magistrates' Courts Act 1978, s. 88 (1)). For example, a wife has an illegitimate child, she and her husband treat the child as a child of their family, the marriage breaks down and the mother cohabits with the child's father. In any matrimonial proceedings between the husband and wife, the child is a child of the husband's family. The fact that the husband was ignorant of the child's paternity will not prevent the child being a child of his family (*W. (R.J.)* v. *W. (S.J.)* (1971)) and the husband thus being liable to maintain the child. In deciding his liability, however, the court must consider, *inter alia*, whether he assumed any responsibility for the child's maintenance and, if so, to what extent and for how long; whether he did so knowing the child was not his own and the liability of anyone else, for example, the father, to maintain the child (Matrimonial Causes Act 1973, s. 25 (3); Domestic Proceedings and Magistrates' Courts Act 1978, s. 3 (3), and see *Roberts* v. *Roberts* (1962)).

A different situation arises if a divorcee, who has custody of the children of the marriage, cohabits with a third party. The non-parent cohabitee is under no corresponding duty to maintain the children of his or her partner's previous marriage, because there must be a marriage between the parties before the child can be a "child of the family." The parent cohabitee and the parent's ex-spouse are alone under a liability to maintain their child. In assessing a parent's liability to maintain, it seems that a cohabitee's means cannot be taken into account (see *Re L.* (1979)). It could be argued, however, that in so far as a cohabitee's support of a partner relieves the partner of self-support, that fact should be relevant when assessing the ability of the partner to maintain his or her children.

3. *The Future*

The existence of one maintenance law for the legitimate child and another, less advantageous, for the illegitimate child has rightly received much criticism. The outcome of the Law Commission's proposals on the abolition of the status of illegitimacy (see *post*, p. 123) and hence the abolition of affiliation proceedings is awaited with interest. The need to establish paternity would, of course, remain.

Any reform of the maintenance law must be linked with a review of illegitimacy as a whole. It may be that English law will follow the example of New Zealand, where the Status of Children Act 1969 provides that the relationship between a person and his father and mother is determined irrespective of whether the father and mother are, or have been, married to each other. The New Zealand legislation, however, is subject to a number of qualifications and does not fully assimilate children born outside marriage with those born within.

CHILD BENEFIT

Child benefit, which replaced family allowances and child tax allowances, is payable to a person who is responsible for one or more children under the age of 16, or under the age of 19 and receiving full-time education at a recognised educational establishment (Child Benefit Act 1975, ss. 1 and 2).

Payment is based on responsibility for a child and not on legitimacy, or even whether the child is a child of the claimant, or not. The question for cohabitees is thus: who is responsible for the child? The Child Benefit Act 1975 provides that a person is "responsible for a child" if he has the child living with him or he is contributing to the cost of providing for the child at a weekly rate which is not less than the weekly rate of child benefit (s. 3). It may be that both cohabitees are "responsible for a child," in which case only one of them is entitled. The Act provides a scheme of priorities (s. 4 and Sched. 2). If benefit has already been paid to a person, he generally has preference over any later claimant (Sched. 2, para. 1). Otherwise, if one person has the child living with him and another is contributing to the child's maintenance, the former has priority (para. 2). If the child is living with cohabitees, both of whom are parents, the mother is entitled (para. 4 (2)). If one cohabitee is a parent and the other is not, the parent is entitled (para. 4 (1)). In other cases, if persons are jointly entitled, for example, if neither is a parent, they must decide between themselves who is to receive benefit. If they do not decide, the Secretary of State will do so (para. 5).

A higher rate of benefit is paid for the first child of single parent families than for the first child of two parent families. To qualify for the higher rate, the claimant must show, *inter alia*, that he is not living with anyone as his spouse. A cohabitation rule thus operates (see Chapter 3 and Child Benefit and Social Security (Fixing and Adjustment of Rates) Regulations 1976). It is proposed that the higher rate should also be payable to single people who are not the child's parents but who are bringing up the child.

INHERITANCE

As a general rule, the parental rights and duties in respect of the illegitimate child are vested solely in the mother (see *ante*, p. 104), even where the mother and father cohabit in a stable relationship. The relationship between father and child is given legal recognition, however, in the event of the death of either of them.

The law of succession was discussed generally in Chapter 5. It is now appropriate to consider the special rules applicable to children. An illegitimate child has always been able to inherit under a will, but the rule used to be that a gift in a will to "children" excluded illegitimate children, unless they were expressly included. The rule was reversed by the Family Law Reform Act 1969, s. 15, so that in any will made after January 1, 1970 a reference to "children" includes illegitimate children, unless the contrary appears. A contrary intention can be inferred, but it is advisable that it should be expressly stated.

If a person dies intestate, there are special rules of succession (see Chapter 5). On the death of an unmarried parent, the estate is held on trust for the children (Administration of Estates Act 1925, ss. 46 and 47).

An illegitimate child has the same succession rights on the intestacy of either parent as the legitimate child (Family Law Reform Act 1969, s. 14 (1)). The rule applies to intestacies after January 1, 1970; before that date the illegitimate child had no rights on the intestacy of his father and could only succeed on the intestacy of his mother if she had no legitimate children. Both parents are entitled to inherit equally on the death of their illegitimate child as on the death of their legitimate child (s. 14 (2)). The rule can be criticised where the father of an illegitimate child has had no contact with, and shown no interest in, the child. The same criticism does not apply if the parents have cohabited as a family with the child and have jointly cared for and maintained him. An illegitimate child is presumed not to have been survived by his father unless the contrary is shown (s. 14 (4)). The rules only apply to inheritance between parents and children. The illegitimate child, unlike the legitimate child, has no rights on the intestate death of other relatives for example, grandparents or brothers and sisters. Likewise, such relatives have no inheritance rights on the illegitimate child's death.

The succession rights of legitimated children are virtually identical to those of the legitimate child. For dispositions made after January 1, 1976, a legitimated child has the same succession rights as if he had been born legitimate (Legitimacy Act 1976, s. 5 (3)).

Illegitimate children cannot inherit titles of honour, neither can a legitimated child (Legitimacy Act 1976, Sched. 1, para. 4 (2)), nor can an adopted child (Children Act 1975, Sched. 1, para. 10). The child of a void marriage who is born after October 28, 1959 and is treated as the legitimate child of his parents (see Legitimacy Act 1976, s. 1, *ante*, p. 101) can succeed to such a title (Legitimacy Act 1976, Sched. 1, para. 4 (1)).

If an illegitimate child inherits nothing from a deceased parent, it has been possible since the Family Law Reform Act 1969 (s. 18) for a claim to be made against the parent's estate. The application must now be made under the Inheritance (Provision for Family and Dependants) Act 1975, s. 1 (1), on the ground that the deceased's will and/or the law of intestacy do not make reasonable financial provision for the applicant (see Chapter 5). The qualified applicants include the deceased's illegitimate child (s. 25 (1)), see, for example, *C. A. v. C. C.* (1978) (*ante*, p. 86), where the illegitimate child was treated equally with his legitimate brother.

REFORM

The Law Commission have published a Working Paper on Illegitimacy proposing major reform of the law. It is not possible in this book to discuss the proposed reforms in detail and so attention will be focused on the Commission's Summary of Provisional Conclusions.

The major proposal is the abolition of the status of illegitimacy and the consequent application, to all children, of the law currently applicable to legitimate children. There would be a number of consequential reforms. Parents of children not born in marriage would have equal parental rights and duties, including guardianship, custody and maintenance. The father would thus be joint guardian of the child and if he outlived the mother would continue as guardian, either solely or jointly with any guardian appointed by the mother. The child of unmarried parents would have the same rights of financial support from both parents as the child of married parents (enforceable under the Guardianship of Minors Acts 1971–73). The father would be liable to maintain the child as a matter of law and not merely in consequence of a court order, so affiliation proceedings would disappear. Children born outside marriage would be able to inherit on the intestacy of all natural relatives, for example, grandparents, brothers and sisters, and these relatives would be able to inherit on the child's intestacy. It is suggested that the word "heir" (whether in connection with a title or not) should not necessarily be limited to children born in marriage. The child's father would be a "parent" for the purposes of adoption and unless the court were to dispense with his agreement, he would be required to agree to the child's adoption. The consent of the father as well as the mother would be required to the child's marriage under the age of 18, if the parents were living together. If they were living apart, only the consent of the parent with custody would be required.

There would remain the need to establish paternity of the child and it is suggested that marriage, including a void marriage, should give rise to a presumption of paternity (replacing the present presumption of legitimacy), but cohabitation should not be treated in the same way as marriage, as prima facie evidence of paternity. In the words of the Commission:

"The value of a 'prima facie evidence rule' lies in its general applicability without further evidence. This condition is satisfied by the marriage presumption, because one starts with a fact about which there is no dispute (that a marriage ceremony has taken place) and then draws the natural inferences from that fact. But cohabitation (or, rather, cohabitation 'as husband and wife', for only such cohabitation can be relevant) is by no means self-proving, especially if there are further statutory definitions going to the durability of the relationship. It also seems to us that once any relevant cohabitation has been proved or admitted, the natural inferences as to the paternity of children would, in the absence of other evidence to the contrary, invariably be drawn.

The formal promotion of cohabitation into 'prima facie evidence' of paternity, as a matter of law, adds virtually nothing" (para. 9.12).

Just as a husband has the right to have himself registered in the register of births as the father of his wife's child, so a procedure is suggested whereby a father who is not married to the child's mother would be able to insist on his name being entered in the births' register, notwithstanding the mother's lack of consent, following the making of a custody or access order in his favour, a maintenance order against him, or a declaration of parentage. At present the court has no power to make a declaration of paternity (*Re J.S.* (1980)). It is proposed that a declaration of parentage should be obtainable without seeking any other order, but only the child himself should have an unqualified right to apply for such a declaration, any other person should be entitled to apply only if the court is satisfied that it is appropriate having regard to the child's welfare. In any proceedings in which paternity is in issue, there should no longer be a rule of law requiring corroboration, nor should the bringing of such proceedings be subject to any time limit.

If the proposal that the status of illegitimacy be abolished becomes law, then one of the advantages of cohabitees marrying, namely to legitimate the children, will be removed. Time alone will tell the impact, if any, that this will have on the incidence of cohabitation.

Further Reading

Bromley, *Family Law* (Butterworths, 5th ed.).

Cretney, *Principles of Family Law* (Sweet and Maxwell, 3rd ed.).

Eekelaar, *Family law and Social Policy* (Weidenfeld and Nicolson).

Sweet and Maxwell's Family Law Statutes (2nd ed.).

Bevan, *The Law Relating to Children* (Butterworths).

Bevan and Parry, *Children Act 1975* (Butterworths).

Hoggett, *Parents and Children* (Sweet and Maxwell).

Law Commission, Working Paper No. 74, Family Law, Illegitimacy (H.M.S.O. 1979).

Levin, "Reforming the Illegitimacy Laws" (1978) 8 Fam. Law 35.

Levin, "Cohabitees—2. Children" (1979) Legal Action Group Bulletin 15.

Report of the Committee on One-Parent Families, Cmnd. 5629.

Report of the Committee on Statutory Maintenance Limits, 1968, Cmnd. 3587.

Terry, *A Guide to the Children Act 1975* (Sweet and Maxwell, 2nd ed.).

7 Marriage and Cohabitation

MARRIAGE BREAKDOWN AND COHABITATION

Many couples who cohabit as man and wife do so because they are unable to marry, one or both of them being already married. The cohabitation may be the cause of the marriage breakdown or it may be a symptom of an already broken marriage. Whatever the reason for the cohabitation, its existence is likely to encourage the end of the marriage by divorce.

Before the coming into force of the Divorce Reform Act 1969 on January 1, 1971, English divorce law was almost entirely fault based, *i.e.* to obtain a divorce "the petitioner" had to show that the other spouse ("the respondent") had committed a matrimonial offence and was thus the "guilty" party, whilst the petitioner was the "innocent" party. The operation of a divorce law akin to the criminal law meant that a spouse who was cohabiting was unlikely to be able to seek a divorce. That remedy was available to the other spouse on the ground of his or her partner's adultery, but many chose not to end the marriage. One consequence was that children born to cohabitees were unable to acquire the status of legitimacy (see Chapter 6).

The 1969 Act (now consolidated in the Matrimonial Causes Act 1973), retained, in part, the matrimonial offence doctrine. There is now only one ground for divorce, namely that the marriage has broken down irretrievably. Irretrievable breakdown must be proved by the petitioner showing one of five facts: that the respondent has committed adultery and the petitioner finds it intolerable to live with the respondent; that the respondent has so behaved that the petitioner cannot reasonably be expected to live with him; that the respondent has deserted the petitioner for at least two years; that the parties have lived apart for at least two years and the respondent agrees to a divorce; or that the parties have lived apart for at least five years (Matrimonial Causes Act 1973, s. 1). The last two facts are "non-fault" based, and a divorce based on five years' separation does not require the agreement of the other spouse. It is thus possible for a "guilty" spouse to obtain a divorce against the wishes of an "innocent" spouse and then marry a cohabitee. This provision was condemned at the time of its introduction as a "Casanova's Charter," the fear being, in particular, that middle-aged wives would be divorced against their wishes and would suffer financial hardship. Those fears have not been realised. It is true that in the first year of the provision's operation it was the basis for one-quarter of the divorce petitions and many cohabitees, particularly elderly couples, who had been living together, were able to marry and thereby legitimate their children. The intention of the Law Commission, that the provision would enable couples to regularise by marriage their "stable illicit unions" (see *Field of Choice*, paras. 33–37), was thus realised, at least in the short term. Once the initial demand by those who had been unable to marry for some years had been met, however, the use of the provision declined. Currently, less than one in ten divorces is granted on this basis. The provision has not proved a "Casanova's Charter" for, of those petitioning, there is an equal number of husbands and wives.

1. *Cohabitation between Spouses*

Cohabitation between the spouses can have important consequences in relation to their divorce. If they cohabit after the event which is being relied upon for the divorce, and do so for more than six months, the cohabitation will bar the granting of a decree in a case based on the respondent's adultery, desertion or either of the separation facts and may bar the granting of a decree if the petitioner's case is based on the respondent's behaviour (Matrimonial Causes Act 1973, s. 2). This is also the case if the parties cohabit for more than six months after the decree nisi but before decree absolute, because the marriage does not end until the decree absolute. So, for example, if as in *Bigg* v. *Bigg* (1977), the parties do so cohabit, the cohabitation operates as a bar to a decree absolute based on adultery.

A similar rule applies during the marriage if either party obtains a magistrates' court order for periodical payments or custody under the Domestic Proceedings and Magistrates' Courts Act 1978. In general, the order is enforceable notwithstanding that the parties are living with each other or resume living with each other, but the order will cease to have effect if they continue or resume living with each other for more than six months after the order (s. 25).

2. *Cohabitation with Another before Divorce*

To what extent does the court, on granting a divorce decree, take into account the fact that one of the spouses is cohabiting with someone else? The question is of particular importance in relation to maintenance and property. Section 25 (1) of the Matrimonial Causes Act 1973 directs the court to have regard to all the circumstances of the case and sets out some of the matters which the court has to consider in deciding whether or not to make a maintenance or property order, and if so, for how much.

The court must consider, *inter alia*, the spouses' financial resources, needs, obligations and responsibilities (s. 25 (1) (*a*) and (*b*)). In so doing, their approach is a practical one. If the husband is being financially supported by another woman, that fact will be taken into account in assessing the husband's ability to provide for his wife, for his own cost of living will be reduced (see, for example, *Ette* v. *Ette* (1965), where the husband was cohabiting rent free with another woman in accommodation which she provided). Likewise if the wife is being financially supported by another man, her financial needs will be that much less (see, for example, *W.* v. *W.* (1975)).

If the husband is supporting another woman, the consequent drain on his financial resources will also be considered (see, for example, *Roberts* v. *Roberts* (1968)), particularly if the woman has children, whether or not they are the man's children.

Although a cohabitee's financial means are relevant under section 25, they should be examined in the general rather than in the particular because, although a cohabitee may be ordered to attend and give evidence, the court has no jurisdiction to order a cohabitee to file an affidavit of means (Matrimonial Causes Rules 1977, r. 77 (5); *Wynne* v. *Wynne* (1980)). That a cohabitee can be ordered to give evidence, but cannot be ordered to disclose fully his or her means, seems contradictory. Surely if the court is going to examine a cohabitee's means, it should have before it as much information as possible, so as to do justice between the spouses. It can be argued in reply, that the assets of a cohabitee are not relevant to the financial claims of the former spouse (see Berkovits (1980)).

Section 25 (1) concludes by requiring the court to exercise its powers *inter alia* having regard to the spouses' conduct. Is cohabitation conduct for this purpose? The courts have interpreted conduct narrowly, so that in the absence of conduct which is "obvious and gross," the court will not penalise a party because of what was formerly regarded as guilt or blame (*Wachtel* v. *Wachtel* (1973)). The type of conduct envisaged is conduct calculated to destroy the marriage where the other spouse is substantially blameless (*Harnett* v. *Harnett* (1973)), *i.e.* conduct such that it would be repugnant to a sense of justice for it not to be taken into account. It is suggested, therefore, that the fact that a spouse is living with someone else and committing adultery will not, in the absence of other conduct, be obvious and gross misconduct (see *Backhouse* v. *Backhouse* (1978) and *cf. Cuzner* v. *Underdown* (1974)).

Having considered all the circumstances, the court has to exercise its powers so as to place the parties in the financial position in which they would have been if the marriage had not broken down. In many cases one income will now have to provide for two families, so inevitably there will be a reduction in the parties' standard of living. A husband who leaves his wife, for whatever reason, and lives with another woman, can expect to have to provide for his wife. This is so, whether or not he plans to remarry. The duty to the first family will limit the income available for the second. A cohabitee, like a second wife, takes her partner subject to the partner's obligations to his first family.

The duty to maintain is, in theory, reciprocal, *i.e.* the spouses come before the court on a basis of equality (*Calderbank* v. *Calderbank* (1975)). This does not mean that their needs are equal. In most cases, the wife will be the one in greater financial need. As a guide, the courts work on the so-called "one-third rule," which is not a rule but a starting point in assessing the wife's entitlement to maintenance, *i.e.* the wife is entitled to one-third of the joint incomes and one-third of the joint capital (*Wachtel* v. *Wachtel* (1973)). Entitlement is subject to the factors in section 25 (1), *i.e.* the parties' financial resources and needs, standard of living, age, length of the marriage, physical or mental disability, contribution to the welfare of the family and loss of any future benefit (for example, pensions). The one-third rule is independent of the spouses' obligations to maintain the children of the family.

The need for one income to provide for two families may mean that one or both of the spouses has to turn to supplementary benefit (see Chapter 3). As they have ceased to be members of the same household, their requirements and resources will no longer be aggregated. The fact that one spouse is receiving benefit does not relieve the other of his obligation to maintain. The courts do not allow a husband to shift his responsibility to maintain his wife and children on to the State. Thus any benefit received will generally be ignored in assessing maintenance. The court, in ordering one spouse to maintain the other, ought not, however, to reduce the payer and his new family below subsistence level. So, in *Barnes* v. *Barnes* (1972) a wife was granted a divorce and her husband was ordered to pay £2 a week for each of the four children of the marriage and a nominal five pence a year for the wife, who was in receipt of social security benefit. The husband later remarried and the order was varied to £1.50 for each child. The wife appealed. The Court of Appeal noted that on the reduction in the order the wife did not suffer financially, because there was a corresponding increase in benefit. It was held, *inter alia*, that in general the court should not have regard to any social security benefits. When, however, the case is one in which the parties' means are so modest that an order would result in the husband being left with inadequate funds to meet his financial commitments, the court may have regard to such benefits. The order was varied by awarding the wife maintenance at £2 per week and leaving the sum payable for each child at £1.50. The same principles apply whether a man is having to divide his resources between his wife and former wife or between his cohabitee and former wife.

The courts have extensive powers on divorce to make property transfer orders, irrespective of who owns the home (Matrimonial Causes Act 1973, s. 24 and see *ante*, p. 14). Increasing emphasis is being placed, by the courts, on the need to provide a home for the parties (see *Martin* v. *Martin* (1977)), and more particularly for the children (see *Hanlon* v. *Hanlon* (1978)). If a husband leaves his wife to cohabit with another woman, he may well find the court transferring the matrimonial home to the wife if she has custody of the children. Custody is the important issue. If the husband cohabits in the matrimonial home and the wife leaves, an order may be made transferring the home to her if she is awarded custody of the children. The husband's maintenace to his wife may be reduced correspondingly.

If one spouse tries to defeat the claims of the other to the home by transferring it into the name of another, for example a cohabitee, the court has power to set aside the transfer and any transfer can be reviewed unless it was made for proper payment (Matrimonial Causes Act 1973, s. 37).

The types of property order available to the court are numerous. It is possible here only to give a general picture. The area is one of the most complex and litigated of family law and one upon which any cohabitee who is involved in divorce proceedings ought to seek legal advice.

3. *Cohabitation with Another after Divorce*

In some cases a spouse does not cohabit until after divorce. An ex-spouse may ask a social worker, "What effect does cohabitation have on an existing maintenance or property order?" The answer depends upon the nature of the original order. A maintenance order in the form of a lump sum is a once and for all payment and is unaffected by later cohabitation. A periodical payments order, however, is a continuing order and therefore subject to later variation or termination. An ex-spouse who remarries loses the benefit of periodical payments in her favour (orders for children are unaffected) except for arrears (Matrimonial Causes Act 1973, s. 28 (1) and (2)). Cohabitation does not have this effect, but a periodical payments order will be subject to the payer's applying for variation of the order in the light of the recipient's cohabitation (Matrimonial Causes Act 1973, s. 31, and see *Wachtel* v. *Wachtel* (1973)). If the court is asked to vary the order it will have regard to all the circumstances, including any change in any of the matters which the court had to consider when making the original order (s. 31 (7), see also *Lewis* v. *Lewis* (1977)). If the payer cohabits, either ex-spouse can apply for a variation in the light of the cohabitation, depending upon whether the cohabitation has increased the payer's obligations or increased his resources.

If an ex-spouse cohabits after divorce but before applying for maintenance, the cohabitation will not bar an application, but will be taken into account when deciding what order, if any, to make. The court may well decide to make a nominal order (see, for example, *W.* v. *W.* (1975)). An ex-spouse who remarries before applying for maintenance, whether in the form of periodical payments or lump sum, is barred from making an application (Matrimonial Causes Act 1973, s. 28 (3)). An ex-spouse who contemplates remarriage is best advised, therefore, to seek a lump sum order (which is unaffected by remarriage) and must apply before remarrying, but not necessarily before cohabiting. Any cohabitation, however, will not be ignored. If an ex-spouse plans to remarry, the effect of remarriage on his financial position will be considered, but if there are no marriage plans the courts will not assess the parties' remarriage prospects when determining maintenance (*Smith* v. *Smith* (1975)).

A property order in favour of an ex-spouse is unaffected by cohabitation or remarriage. It is a once and for all order and as such cannot be varied or terminated. A property order is thus akin to a lump sum maintenance order, and an ex-spouse in whose favour such an order is made, is in a better position in the event of remarriage or cohabitation, than an ex-spouse with a periodical payments order. It remains important, however, to apply for the order before remarrying, for no application is possible after remarriage (Matrimonial Causes Act 1973, s. 28 (3)). Cohabitation does not bar an application but will be considered.

4. *Children*

Custody

In divorce proceedings, the court must not make the decree absolute unless it is satisfied that the arrangements for the welfare of the "children of the family" are satisfactory, or the best that can be devised in the circumstances, or that it is impracticable to make any such arrangements (Matrimonial Causes Act 1973, s. 41 (1)). The court is therefore under a duty to consider the children's future and, in deciding what order to make for their custody, the court must regard the children's welfare as "the first and paramount consideration" (Guardianship of Minors Act 1971, s. 1).

If either of the parties to the divorce is cohabiting, the cohabitation will be a factor to be taken into account when deciding custody. The conduct of the parties, however, is relevant only in so far as it relates to the child's welfare. At one time the courts considered the parties' conduct towards each other, so, for example, to deny an adulterous mother any claim to custody. Such is no longer the case (see, for example, *Willoughby* v. *Willoughby* (1951)). The courts are no longer concerned with doing justice between the parties (see, for example, *S. (B.D.)* v. *S. (D.J.)* (1977) and *Re K.* (1976) and *cf. Re L.* (1962)). Adultery by one parent is relevant only in so far as it is likely to have an effect on the children. The same principle applies if there is a custody dispute during marriage and one of the parents is cohabiting. Thus in *Re K.* the wife of a clergyman formed an adulterous relationship with another man and they bought a house in joint names. The husband refused to divorce the wife so she applied for custody of the children in order to take them with her when she went to live with the other man. The court decided that the children's welfare was first and paramount and the court should not balance that welfare against the wishes of an unimpeachable parent or against the justice of the case as between the parents. The mother was an excellent mother and she was awarded custody.

The court will investigate the stability of the cohabitation and whether or not there is any possibility of the parents being reconciled. It will also consider the suitability of the cohabitee as a parent substitute (see *Re F.* (1969) and *Hutchinson* v. *Hutchinson* (1978)). To this end the cohabitee will be required to attend the custody hearing (*S.* v. *S.* (1972)).

Surname

One problem of particular significance on divorce is that which occurs when the wife has been awarded custody and forms a relationship with another man, and she wishes to change her children's surname to that of her new partner. The problem usually arises on remarriage but also occurs if the wife cohabits. It was settled law that the mother had no right to change her children's surname except with the father's consent or with leave of the court (see *Re T.* (1962), *Y.* v. *Y.* (1973), *Re W. G.* (1976), Matrimonial Causes Rules 1977, r. 92 (8)). The courts rarely gave leave for change except where it was felt that a complete severance from the father was desirable. Recent cases suggest some change in judicial attitudes and a greater preparedness to permit a unilateral change of name (see *Crick* v. *Crick* (1977), *R.* v. *R.* (1978), *D.* v. *B.* (1979)). The change of attitude has allowed more attention to be paid to what is best for the child, for example, the effect of being known by a different surname from brothers and sisters and the embarrassment this can cause at school.

The matter, however, is by no means settled (see *L.* v. *F.* (1978), *W.* v. *A.* (1981)), and the courts are likely to be particularly reluctant to sanction a change if the mother and her new partner are not married. Much will depend upon the stability of the cohabitation, as for example in *R.* v. *R.* (1978), where the court found a strong relationship between the mother and her cohabitee. The mother had been granted custody of the three eldest children on divorce and they were known by her cohabitee's surname. She later applied for custody of the youngest child who had been living with his father since the divorce. The Court of Appeal held that in deciding the custody of the child, the fact that the three eldest children had taken the cohabitee's surname was not of significance, it was merely more convenient that they should be known by that name. The observations in that case were subsequently seen, however, as being confined to their context and not establishing a general proposition. In *W.* v. *A.* (1981), the Court of Appeal stressed that the matter is one of discretion for the judge. The child's welfare is the first and paramount consideration. A change of name is an important matter so far as the child's welfare is concerned and a change will not be sanctioned lightly.

CONSORTIUM

Marriage confers upon the spouses mutual rights and duties, the chief of which is a mutual duty to live together or "cohabit"; thus each has the right to the other's "consortium." The law sees cohabitation and the sharing of lives and a home as the essence of marriage and recognises rights and duties arising from the cohabitation; for example, the "right" to intercourse (see *post*, p. 138), the duty to maintain (see *ante*, p. 36). None of these apply to the unmarried, even though the term cohabitation is frequently used to describe a stable relationship outside marriage.

At one time the law would enforce the duty to cohabit by granting a deserted spouse a decree of restitution of conjugal rights, requiring the deserting spouse to return. Such actions have been abolished (Matrimonial Proceedings and Property Act 1970, s. 20). The law still recognises the matrimonial "offence" of desertion, however, and the deserted spouse can base a claim on desertion in divorce proceedings or in proceedings for maintenance during marriage. No such obligation exists between cohabitees.

A spouse whose right to consortium had been interfered with by a third party used to be able to bring an action for enticement, seduction and harbouring, but such actions have also been abolished (Law Reform (Miscellaneous Provisions) Act 1970, s. 5), as has a husband's right to claim damages for adultery from a co-respondent in divorce proceedings (s. 4). A husband, however, can still bring an action for loss of consortium against a third party who wrongfully injures his wife, resulting in the loss of her services (*Cutts* v. *Chumley* (1967)). No such action is available to a cohabitee.

Further Reading

Bromley, *Family Law* (Butterworths, 5th ed.).

Cretney, *Principles of Family Law* (Sweet and Maxwell, 3rd ed.).

Eekelaar, *Family Law and Social Policy* (Weidenfeld and Nicolson).

Sweet and Maxwell's Family Law Statutes (2nd ed.).

Berkovits, "Compelling Disclosure of 'Invisible' Assets upon Divorce" (1980) 130 N.L.J. 648.

Evans, "Changing A Child's Name After Re-Marriage" (1978) 8 Fam. Law 112.

Law Commission, *Reform of the Grounds of Divorce. The Field of Choice,* Cmnd. 3123.

Law Commission, *The Financial Consequences of Divorce: The Basic Policy* (Law Com. No. 103).

Parry, "Changing A Child's Name After Re-Marriage: A Reply" (1978) 8 Fam. Law 253.

8 Other Consequences

The legal responsibilities and liabilities arising as a result of cohabitation are not limited to those already discussed, nor do they necessarily fit within the preceding chapters. Other responsibilities are owed by cohabitees to each other and to third parties. Consideration will now be given to some of them.

CONTRACTS

A cohabitee can enter into a contract with a third party or with his or her partner, as can a spouse. Does the law attach any special status to their contractual capacity in the light of the cohabitation?

1. *Contracts with Others*

A wife who is cohabiting with her husband is presumed to have his authority to pledge his credit for necessary goods and services (*Phillipson* v. *Hayter* (1870)) for example, food, clothing and household goods. The agency arises out of the cohabitation and can therefore be said to apply to an unmarried couple who are cohabiting as husband and wife (*Blades* v. *Free* (1829)). As the woman is regarded as her partner's agent, he is liable to the supplier.

If a man leads a supplier to believe that his cohabitee is acting as his agent, for example, by paying for goods which she has ordered, he will be regarded as holding her out as his agent. If she orders further goods from that supplier, her partner will be liable to the supplier for the price (*Ryan* v. *Sams* (1848)).

2. *Contracts between Cohabitees*

Cohabitees are free to enter into contracts with each other but, as with contracts between spouses, any such contract may be regarded as an agreement which was not intended to be legally binding (*Balfour* v.

Balfour (1919))) *i.e.* the parties did not intend to create a legal relationship and the agreement is therefore unenforceable. In order to overcome this difficulty, the agreement should make it clear that the parties intend to create a legally enforceable agreement. An agreement in the case of a family cohabitation, for example between a brother and sister, is likely to be unenforceable on this basis, unless there is clear evidence to the contrary. An agreement will be enforceable if it is clearly a business agreement, or if the parties have separated or are about to separate (*Merritt* v. *Merritt* (1970)).

One type of contract between cohabitees calls for special comment, namely a "cohabitation contract," *i.e.* an agreement to cohabit and to provide for the parties' rights on breakdown of cohabitation. In this respect cohabitees are in a different position from spouses. Marriage is certain, the spouses have contracted a marriage evidenced by a marriage ceremony. Cohabitation is uncertain and is not self-evident. To some cohabitees the lack of ties and commitments is the advantage of cohabitation, whereas others may wish to regularise their relationship. Should they be able to enter into an agreement to that effect? A form of such an agreement has been suggested (see Gray (1973)) but its validity has never been upheld. As with any contract between cohabitees, it might be argued that the agreement was not intended to be legally binding. Should it be accepted that a cohabitation contract was intended to create a legal relationship, the courts may refuse to enforce it on the basis that it is an immoral contract (see Dwyer (1977)) and thus illegal (see, for example, *Walker* v. *Perkins* (1794)).

It is suggested that a distinction must be drawn between a contract, the purpose of which is to provide for a sexual relationship and a contract to regulate a stable cohabitation outside marriage. Whilst the former may be viewed as contrary to public policy (see Lord Wright in *Fender* v. *St. John Mildmay* (1937), *ante*, p. 38 and further examples given by Poulter (1974)) the same need not be said of the latter. If the agreement is a genuine attempt by the parties to regulate their obligations towards each other and their children, for example by way of maintenance or the provision of a home, rather than provision for payment for a sexual relationship, the courts should give consideration to the agreement. In so doing, they should have a discretion whether or not to give effect to the agreement, so that it would not be enforced if to do so would not be in the interests of justice, for example, if the agreement were not in the children's interests.

The law already accepts contracts for the maintenance of illegitimate children as not being contrary to public policy (see Chapter 6) and has given effect to agreements, express and implied, over property rights (see Chapter 2). It is suggested that this acceptance should extend to cohabitation contracts, on the basis that judicial statements against such acceptance no longer reflect society's changed attitude to unmarried partnerships.

It may be possible to extend generally the recognition already given to implied agreements with regard to ownership of the home, so that a cohabitee who cohabits to his detriment on the understanding that he would be supported, has a "quasi-contractual" claim, *i.e.* a claim which, although not contractual, arises as if from a contract.

It is not suggested that an agreement to live together could be enforced but that an agreement which provides for the parties' obligations in the event of breakdown of the cohabitation could be enforced. The present law may "deter couples who do not wish to be subject to the rights and duties attached by law to the status of marriage from making proper arrangements to govern the financial and other consequences of their relationship" (Law Commission). In so saying, the Law Commission express the initial view "that it might be appropriate at some stage to examine, with a view to reform, the rules now governing contracts between couples who live together outside marriage, since it is perhaps in that area that the law is most uncertain and outdated" (Law Com. No. 97, para. 2.32).

TORT

A tort, in general terms, is a civil wrong giving rise to a claim for damages, not being merely a breach of contract, for example, negligence, defamation. In an action in tort, a cohabitee can sue, and be sued, in the same way as any other individual. For the purpose of actions between cohabitees, no special status is conferred upon them as a result of the cohabitation. Likewise, in actions between spouses, the parties are generally treated as though they are not married (Law Reform (Husband and Wife) Act 1962, s. 1). No special rules of legal unity apply in actions against a married person, but in the law of defamation (*i.e.* libel and slander) a communication by one spouse to the other, but not by one cohabitee to the other, of a defamatory statement of a third party is not a publication and so there is no liability (*Wennhak* v. *Morgan* (1888)). The communication of a defamation of one spouse, or one cohabitee, to the other by a third party is a publication so as to render the third party liable (*Wenman* v. *Ash* (1853)).

CRIMINAL LAW

The criminal law recognises, for certain purposes, the status of a married person.

1. Rape

As a general rule, a husband cannot be guilty of raping his wife (*R.* v. *Miller* (1954)). A man commits rape if he has unlawful sexual intercourse with a woman without her consent and he knows she does not consent or is reckless as to whether she consents (Sexual Offences Act 1956, s. 1, as amended by Sexual Offences (Amendment) Act 1976, s. 1). By the contract of marriage the wife is under a duty to cohabit, an essential part of which is consent to sexual intercourse. No such consent is inferred as a result of cohabitation, so a man living with a woman as her husband may be guilty of raping her. A cohabitee wishing to prove rape against her partner is, of course, faced with the considerable burden of proving that the act of intercourse was without her consent.

2. Conspiracy

A husband and wife cannot be guilty of conspiring together (*Mawji* v. *R.* (1957); Criminal Law Act 1977, s. 2 (2) (*a*)) but cohabitees can.

3. Marital Coercion

The defence of marital coercion which may be available to a wife who proves that an offence was committed in the presence of, and under the coercion of, her husband (Criminal Justice Act 1925, s. 47) is, by its nature, not available to a female cohabitee.

4. Evidence

The rule that one spouse cannot generally be compelled to give evidence against the other (*Hoskyn* v. *Metropolitan Police Commissioner* (1978)) does not apply to cohabitees. Likewise, spouses are generally not competent to testify against one another, whereas cohabitees are.

BANKRUPTCY

Certain rules of bankruptcy which apply when a spouse becomes bankrupt do not apply on the bankruptcy of a cohabitee. So, for example, the claim of a spouse for certain loans to the bankrupt is deferred until the claims of other creditors have been paid (Bankruptcy Act 1914, s. 36). Conversely the provisions of the Bankruptcy Act 1914, whereby a settlement of property may be set aside on the settlor's bankruptcy, do not apply to marriage settlements (s. 42).

INSURANCE

The Life Assurance Act 1774, s. 1, requires the person for whose benefit a life assurance policy is made to have an insurable interest in the life of the assured; any policy made contrary to this requirement is void. Marriage, but not cohabitation, is seen as giving the parties an insurable interest in the life of each other without the need to prove financial loss (*Griffiths* v. *Fleming* (1909); Married Women's Property Act 1882, s. 11).

Relationships other than that of husband and wife, do not constitute an insurable interest unless there is a financial interest (*Halford* v. *Kymer* (1830)), capable of valuation in money and founded on a legally recognised obligation. The amount of the insurable interest will be the loss which the person, for whose benefit the assurance is taken, will sustain by reason of the assured's death.

It is open to argument that a cohabitee, who is supported financially by his or her partner, has an insurable interest in the other's life, up to the amount of financial support which will be lost by the assured's death. In so far as the law indirectly recognises a support obligation between cohabitees (see *ante*, p. 28), there will be the loss of a benefit which the law recognises as one of financial value. There will be the difficulty, of course, of establishing the support obligation and the resulting financial loss. Such an obligation is recognised, for example, for purposes of claims under the Inheritance (Provision for Family and Dependants) Act 1975 (see Chapter 5) on the basis of dependence. Would not a life assurance policy be merely providing for the same dependence? Care would need to be taken with the drawing up of the policy and the appropriate legal and insurance advice taken.

NATIONALITY

A woman who is not a citizen of the United Kingdom and Colonies and who marries a United Kingdom citizen can acquire such citizenship by registration (British Nationality Act 1948, s. 6 (2)). Cohabitation with a United Kingdom citizen confers no such right.

Anyone born within the United Kingdom is a United Kingdom citizen by birth regardless of his parents' nationality or their marital status (1948 Act, s. 4). If United Kingdom citizenship is claimed by descent rather than by birth, the claim will depend upon the father's citizenship and the parents' marital status. Citizenship by descent is acquired if the child's father is a United Kingdom citizen at the child's birth (1948 Act, s. 5), but "father" means father of a legitimate or legitimated child (1948 Act, ss. 32 (2) and 23), so a child of unmarried parents cannot claim citizenship by descent from the father. Moreover, there is no citizenship by descent through the mother, so if the mother is a United Kingdom citizen the child still cannot claim citizenship by descent.

The parents (or guardians) of a legitimate child born abroad, whose father is not a United Kingdom citizen but whose mother is, may apply for the child to be registered as a United Kingdom citizen (1948 Act, s. 7 (1)). This provision does not apply to illegitimate children (1948 Act, s. 32 (2)). There are only two circumstances in which an illegitimate child born abroad may acquire citizenship. First, by registration "in special circumstances" under s. 7 (2) of the 1948 Act. In such circumstances the Home Secretary has a discretion to register any "minor" as a United Kingdom citizen. The term "minor" includes illegitimate children and a child's illegitimacy can be a factor in determining "special circumstances." The child must not have reached the age of majority (1948 Act, s. 32 (1)). Second, if the child is stateless and his mother was a United Kingdom citizen at his birth, an application for registration as a United Kingdom citizen may be made by the child or on his behalf (British Nationality (No. 2) Act 1964, s. 1 (1) (a) and (2)). Registration is not dependent upon the Home Secretary's discretion and can be made after the child has reached the age of majority.

The Law Commission see a strong argument in favour of allowing a child, born abroad to a mother who is a United Kingdom citizen, to acquire that citizenship from her (Law Com. Working Paper No. 74, para. 7.7). This would allow the legitimate child to acquire citizenship from either parent. It is also proposed to remove the discrimination against illegitimate children, so as to allow a child, born abroad out of wedlock, to be a United Kingdom citizen by descent either from his mother or from his father (para. 7.10).

A Green Paper on nationality law was published in 1977 with a view to rationalising citizenship. This was followed by a White Paper published in July 1980, which is intended to be a basis for future legislation. New provisions are proposed to replace those in the 1948 Act discussed above, and a Nationality Bill has been introduced, setting out the changes in the law of nationality.

IMMIGRATION

A person's right to enter and live in the United Kingdom depends upon his being a "patrial" within the meaning of the Immigration Act 1971, ss. 1 and 2. A woman who is a Commonwealth citizen and is the wife of a patrial will also be a patrial (1971 Act, s. 2 (2)). The rule does not apply to a cohabitee.

A Commonwealth citizen born to, or legally adopted by, a parent who is a United Kingdom citizen by birth in the United Kingdom, is a patrial (1971 Act, s. 2 (1) (*d*)). "Parent" includes the mother, but not the father, of an illegitimate child (1971 Act, s. 2 (3) (*a*)).

If a person is settled in the United Kingdom or is admitted for settlement, that person's wife will be admitted for settlement. A woman who has been living in permanent association with a man may be admitted as if she were his wife, "due account being taken of any local custom or tradition tending to establish the permanence of the association," but there is no right of entry. The man must be settled here and able and willing to support her and provide adequate accommodation for her (Immigration Rules). The Rules now provide that a woman will not be admitted under this provision unless any previous marriage by either party has permanently broken down. She will also not be admitted if the man has already been joined by his wife, or if another cohabitee has already been admitted under this provision, irrespective of whether or not the relationship still subsists.

DOMICILE

A person's domicile can be described in general terms as his home and the law of the domicile generally governs questions of status, for example, capacity to marry.

One consequence of the doctrine of unity of marriage was that a wife was regarded as taking her husband's domicile on marriage and her domicile remained dependent on his throughout the marriage. The rule was changed by the Domicile and Matrimonial Proceedings Act 1973, s. 1, and since January 1, 1974 a wife's domicile has been ascertained independently of her husband's. A wife is thus treated the same as a cohabitee.

Cohabitation remains distinct from marriage so far as the domicile of children is concerned. A person cannot acquire an independent domicile until he attains the age of 16 or marries under that age (Domicile and Matrimonial Proceedings Act 1973, s. 3). At birth a child acquires a domicile of origin. A legitimate child's domicile of origin is that of his father, whereas an illegitimate child takes his domicile of origin from his mother (*Udny* v. *Udny* (1869)). Until a child reaches 16 (or marries) his domicile changes (to a domicile of dependency) with that of his father, if he is legitimate, and with that of his mother, if he is illegitimate. (There is an exception if his parents are living apart, in which case a legitimate child's domicile of dependency is that of his mother if he has his home with her—1973 Act, s. 4.) The children of cohabitees will therefore take their mother's domicile and not their father's domicile.

The Law Commission have tentatively proposed a new rule in relation to all children, namely that a child's domicile of origin should be that of his mother and thereafter her domicile should control the child's domicile of dependence. If the parents live apart and the child lives with the father, the child's domicile of dependence should be that of his father (Law Com. Working Paper No. 74, paras. 8.3 to 8.5).

Further Reading

Bromley, *Family Law* (Butterworths, 5th ed.).
Cretney, *Principles of Family Law* (Sweet and Maxwell, 3rd ed.).
Eekelaar, *Family Law and Social Policy* (Weidenfeld and Nicolson).
Sweet and Maxwell's Family Law Statutes (2nd ed.).
British Nationality Law: Discussion of possible changes, Cmnd. 6795 (1977).
British Nationality Law, Cmnd. 7987.
Criminal Law Revision Committee, Working Paper on Sexual Offences (H.M.S.O. 1980).
Dwyer, "Immoral Contracts" (1977) 93 L.Q.R. 386.
Gray, "A New Lease of Life" (1973) 123 N.L.J. 591, 596.
Immigration Rules (H.C. 394, 1979–80).
Law Commission, Fourteenth Annual Report 1978–1979 (Law Com. No. 97).
Law Commission, Working Paper No. 74, Family Law, Illegitimacy (H.M.S.O. 1979).
Poulter, "Cohabitation Contracts and Public Policy" (1974) 124 N.L.J. 999, 1034.

9 Conclusion

Those who live together outside marriage have not, as yet, achieved the same legal recognition as those who live together within it. Nevertheless, some judicial and statutory recognition is being given to cohabitation, although its extent is uncertain and inconsistent. The law recognises, for example, contributions towards the acquisition of the home and its contents, and the right of a cohabitee to live in the home free from violence. A cohabitee, unlike a spouse, however, has no right, as such, to maintenance and no right to a home by virtue of the relationship alone. Yet, for supplementary benefit purposes, a couple living together as husband and wife are treated in the same way as spouses.

The uncertainty and inconsistency of recognition is due to its having been secured on an ad hoc basis, with a view to achieving justice in the particular context and with little thought for public policy and the social implications. The tendency has been to treat cohabitees as spouses, not, it seems, because of a desire to equate marriage and cohabitation, but to avoid the necessity for considering what policy should apply to the law relating to cohabitation. Recognition, in so far as it is given, is given in part on the basis of living together as husband and wife (for example, entitlement to supplementary benefit and protection from violence), in part on the basis of the parties' agreed intention (rights in the home) and in part on the basis of dependency (rights on death). If recognition is to be given to cohabitation, should the law continue to develop on an ad hoc basis or should the legal test be one of status, contract or dependence?

Recognition of the status of cohabitee means the granting of rights solely on the strength of cohabitation. Such an approach has been criticised because it can produce unjust results, for example, where one cohabitee, whether the woman or the man, makes no financial or physical contribution to the home acquired by the other, chooses freely a homebound role rather than work and lives in comfort through the other's support with no agreement on the creation of mutual rights and obligations (see Zuckerman (1980)).

One major problem with the status approach to cohabitation lies in identifying the types of cohabitation to which recognition is to be given. The tendency has been to recognise relationships in which the parties have performed the roles of husband and wife. To define cohabitation in terms of living together as husband and wife would necessitate a close investigation of each relationship to ascertain whether or not the relationship has the necessary personal qualities. This would produce all the difficulties associated with the operation of a cohabitation rule (see Chapter 3) and the danger of encouraging litigation in order to ascertain the types of relationship encompassed by the definition. A definition in terms of marriage would exclude family cohabitations and, presumably, homosexual cohabitations (see Chapter 1).

It has been suggested that cohabitation for a specified minimum period justifies equating the relationship with marriage (see, for example, Mental Health Act 1959, s. 49 (6)). In Tasmania, the Maintenance Act 1967 enables a "*de facto* wife" who has lived with her "*de facto* husband" for at least one year to apply, in certain circumstances, for maintenance. The British Columbia Family Relations Act 1978 provides, in relation to maintenance and support obligations, that "spouse" includes "a man or woman not married to each other, who lived together as husband and wife for a period of not less than 2 years, where an application under this Act is made by one of them against the other not more than 1 year after the date they ceased living together as husband and wife."

The logical extension would be to apply the matrimonial law to those who live together as husband and wife. It has been argued that the power of the matrimonial courts to adjust the balance between the parties should be exercisable whenever parties to a relationship have been fulfilling roles equivalent to the marital roles (Eekelaar (1975)). To do so, however, would seem to undermine marriage if those who do not marry are to be treated identically to those who do. The law has encouraged marriage and discouraged cohabitation, in the words of one judge:

> "It is the ceremony of marriage and the sanctity of marriage which count; rights, duties and obligations begin on the marriage and not before. It is a complete cheapening of the marriage relationship, which I believe, and I am sure many share this belief, is essential to the well-being of our society as we understand it, to suggest that pre-marital periods, ... should, as it were, by a doctrine of relation back of matrimony, be taken as part of marriage to count in favour of the wife performing, as it is put, 'wifely duties before marriage.'" (Sir George Baker in *Campbell* v. *Campbell* (1977).)

The encouragement of marriage has resulted in resistance to any formulation of a basis of recognition for cohabitation, yet there is no need to assimilate the rights of spouses and the rights of cohabitees. The tendency to do so has meant that cohabitation has been seen as a challenge to marriage and therefore undesirable. Cohabitation is not becoming a replacement for marriage. Once it is seen as an alternative to marriage, and one which does not constitute a threat to marriage, the basis for recognition could be developed accordingly.

Discussion so far has concentrated on cohabitation giving rise to a status. Does such a status accord with the expectations of those who cohabit? People marry in the knowledge and expectation of the rights and obligations imposed by marriage. Is it right that those who cohabit in order to be free of marital rights and obligations should have rights and obligations thrust upon them? It can be argued that any further extension of legal recognition is unnecessary and undesirable.

An alternative would be to regard the rights of cohabitees as a matter of contract rather than a matter of status so that the law should only confer rights and obligations if such was the parties' agreed intention. The law's reluctance to recognise any such agreement was discussed in Chapter 8 and it was there suggested that a distinction should be drawn between an agreement for a sexual purpose and an agreement to regulate a stable cohabitation outside marriage. If the agreement is a genuine attempt to regulate the parties' obligations the courts should be prepared to give effect to it unless to do so would not be in the interests of justice, for example, if the parties were of unequal bargaining power.

In the United States of America the courts are prepared to enforce agreements between cohabitees unless the agreement is based on unlawful consideration. In the celebrated case of *Marvin* v. *Marvin* (1976), the California Supreme Court held that:

"The fact that a man and woman live together without marriage, and engage in sexual relationship, does not in itself invalidate agreements between them related to their earnings, property or expenses. Neither is such an agreement invalid merely because the parties may have contemplated the creation or continuation of a non-marital relationship when they entered into it. Agreements between non-marital partners fail only to the extent that they rest upon a consideration of meretricious sexual services."

The court also said that a claim could be upheld on the basis of an implied contract, partnership, or equitable remedies. The claim of Lee Marvin's cohabitee for compensation for the career she had given up so as to live with Mr. Marvin was sent back to the trial court to decide whether or not there had been a contract between the parties. The court ultimately decided that there was no express or implied contract but awarded her an equitable remedy of $104,000 for rehabilitation purposes.

The American courts accept that couples living together outside marriage do have rights arising from their relationship, albeit that the compensation awarded in respect of these rights may be less than would have been awarded had they been married. There is a recognition of cohabitation without equating it with marriage.

It has been argued by some that parties should be allowed to choose the terms of their marriage contract and define the terms of their relationship. In effect the cohabitation contract would replace marriage. Such a fundamental change in our social policy is not currently realistic, but there is a much stronger case for a review of the rules applicable to contracts between couples who live together outside marriage. The law already indirectly recognises such contracts as a means of conferring support rights and property rights, see for example the contractual licence (*Tanner* v. *Tanner, ante*, p. 26).

One difficulty with cohabitation contracts is that where the relationship has lasted for a considerable time the parties are unlikely to have contracted in the light of changing circumstances. Such a problem is not insurmountable. The courts constantly deal with variation of maintenance orders and agreements between spouses in the light of changed circumstances. It is unnecessary and impractical for the parties to have to contract in detailed terms. Indeed recognition could be given to implied agreements as well as express agreements, as already occurs with regard to interests in the home (see, for example, *Cooke* v. *Head, ante*, p. 17) so that a party who cohabits to his or her detriment on the understanding that he or she would be supported would be entitled to some support.

One suggestion has been to base rights on "mutual interdependence" in a stable relationship (see Pearl (1978)) on the basis that a more radical reappraisal of the legal position is unlikely in the immediate future. The law already gives statutory recognition to dependency rather than cohabitation in the Inheritance (Provision for Family and Dependants) Act 1975 (see Chapter 5). Such a test extends rights to dependants whether or not they live together as husband and wife. Thus a test of dependency would extend rights and obligations to family cohabitations and, logically, homosexual cohabitations where there is a mutual interdependence (see Chapter 1).

A similar argument advocates the extension of rights and obligations where a relationship has reduced one party, usually, but not necessarily, the woman, to a position of dependency, normally because of responsibilities for children (Oliver (1978)).

A problem common to any test of recognition of cohabitation is the significance, if any, to be attached to the marital status of either party to the cohabitation. By giving recognition to a married person's extra-marital relationship is not the law moving away from accepting marriage as being a monogamous union and accepting instead a form of polygamy?

The development of the law relating to unmarried couples in other countries, particularly common law countries, is worthy of note. When considering other countries' approach to cohabitation, consideration must be given to the extent to which the approach is based on cultural policies and philosophies which are different from our own. There does seem to be some truth in the saying that what is happening in America today happens in England tomorrow. America has applied to cohabitation, principles of business partnerships (see, for example, *Re Estate of Thornton* (1972)) contract, trusts, and equitable remedies, without necessarily equating marriage and cohabitation (see *Marvin* v. *Marvin*, above). The law can thereby recognise cohabitation whilst supporting marriage. The Canadian courts have held that property acquired during cohabitation should be divided between the parties on breakdown of the relationship so, for example, the fact that the legal title to the home is vested in the man will not prevent the finding of a constructive trust if there is a common intention that the beneficial interest in the home should belong to both parties (*Dwyer* v. *Love* (1976)). English law has developed on similar lines, leaving innovation largely to the judges through the concepts of the trust, the licence, the contract and estoppel (see Chapter 2).

It has been argued that the current practice of judicial discretion is preferable to a legislative code of rights for cohabitees (see Zuckerman (1980)). This allows the courts to give effect to rights and obligations created by the parties themselves through agreement and other relevant conduct in accordance with recognised legal principles thereby minimising uncertainty. Such an approach avoids the difficulties of definition associated with the status approach, which can in addition be seen as undesirable because it treats those who have chosen not to marry as if they had married.

It seems likely that English law will continue to develop as before and concentrate on achieving justice in the particular context, as, and when, it arises, notwithstanding the inconsistencies and uncertainties of such an approach and the failure to give overall consideration to the policies and principles relating to cohabitation.

The Law Commission, as part of their duty to keep the law under review, have given consideration to the legal position of unmarried couples who live together as husband and wife (see Law Com. No. 97, para. 2.32). The Commission note the inconsistent approach in the different statutory provisions and the risk that difficulties of interpretation will occur. Reform and rationalisation of the law is seen as involving enormous problems, not least because of the social and financial implications. The Commission have considered an internal study paper which summarises the English law and reforms in other countries. Their initial view is that a review of the rules governing contracts between couples who live together outside marriage might be appropriate (see *ante*, p. 137) but they decline to say when, if at all, this could be done, and whether or not it should be seen as a preliminary to a more general review.

In one respect the Law Commission are definite that reform of the law is warranted. Discrimination against children on the ground of their parents' marital status cannot be justified and the Law Commission's proposals on the removal of such discrimination are to be welcomed (see Chapter 6). The proposals are in line with reforms already made in other countries, for example, Norway (since 1915) and Sweden. The New Zealand Status of Children Act 1969 provides that "... the relationship between every person and his father and mother shall be determined irrespective of whether the father and mother are or have been married to each other, and all other relationships shall be determined accordingly." The United Kingdom has signed the European Convention on the legal status of children born out of wedlock, which commits contracting States to the principle of equal maintenance and succession rights for all children and to the principle of greater paternal custody and access rights.

The problem remains, however, with regard to cohabitees' obligations and rights between themselves and to third parties. As the law recognises cohabitation, is it not time for a clear and comprehensive review of the mutual rights and obligations of cohabitees? Conferring a status on cohabitees does not necessitate that status being identical to that of spouse. The acceptance of cohabitation suggests a need for an alternative to marriage, not an assimilation of cohabitation and marriage. There is a need for the development of clear principles upon which to base the legal recognition so that those who cohabit can be advised with certainty, first whether or not their relationship is one of cohabitation and second, if it is, the legal rights and obligations arising from that relationship.

Further Reading

Bromley, *Family Law* (Butterworths, 5th ed.).

Cretney, *Principles of Family Law* (Sweet and Maxwell, 3rd ed.).

Eekelaar, *Family Law and Social Policy* (Weidenfeld and Nicolson).

Sweet and Maxwell's Family Law Statutes (2nd ed.).

Bates, "Trusts and Extra-Marital Cohabitation: An Australian Perspective" (1980) Conv. 124.

Blake, "To Marry or Not to Marry?" (1980) 10 Fam. Law 29.

Eekelaar, "The Place of Divorce in Family Law's New Role" (1975) 38 M.L.R. 241.

Eekelaar and Katz, *Marriage and Cohabitation in Contemporary Societies—An Area of Legal, Social and Ethical Change—An International and Interdisciplinary Study* (Butterworths).

Fleischmann, "Marriage by Contract: Defining the Terms of Relationship" (1974) 8 Fam. Law Quarterly 27.

Freeman and Lyon, "Towards a Justification of Rights of Cohabitees" (1980) 130 N.L.J. 228.

Law Commission, Fourteenth Annual Report 1978–79 (Law Com. No. 97).

Oliver, "The Mistress in Law" (1978) 31 Current Legal Problems 81.

Pearl, "The Legal Implications of a Relationship Outside Marriage" (1978) C.L.J. 252.

Zuckerman, "Formality and the Family—Reform and Status Quo" (1980) 96 L.Q.R. 248.

INDEX